SETTING US FREE
AN UNEXPECTED JOURNEY OF GRACE

NICK J. STUMBO
Foreword by **Dr. Ted Roberts**

ENDORSEMENTS

"Nick is a warrior with a uniquely passionate heart for God! His words will stir your heart and give courage to your soul, no matter what you may be battling. I recommend that you read Nick's book with an open heart, because he has a delightful way with words and is a creative thinker. Personal application of the exercises and tools will help you understand yourself much better and come to grips with why you do what you do."

Dr. Ted Roberts | *Pure Desire Ministries International*

"I can feel the smile on my face right now as I envision readers holding the story of what God has done in Nick Stumbo's life in their hands. What God has brought to pass in his life over the past few years is a contagious story of redemption and beauty. Nick is a man who is walking in wholeness and holiness, and it is demonstrating itself in how he leads and how he lives. He walks the talk, and what he writes is absolutely worth reading. I highly recommend his words and his story to all who will take the time to read it."

Matt Bota | *Lead Pastor, RockPointe Church*

SETTING US FREE
AN UNEXPECTED JOURNEY OF GRACE
by Nick Stumbo

© 2015 by Nick Stumbo

Published by
Pure Desire Ministries International
www.puredesire.org | Gresham, Oregon | June 2015

ISBN 978-0-9839993-7-9

Content editing by Heather Kolb

Cover design, interior design, and typesetting by Elisabeth Windsor

To my wife
who walked with me through some
dark woods until we emerged into
the bright sun of a new day

TABLE OF CONTENTS

FOREWORD

Usually my first impressions of someone are not very accurate. But when I first met Nick, I sensed the Holy Spirit was up to something profound, so I listened and watched carefully. I was getting the usual signals of a terrified pastor who didn't want to be sitting in my office. His wife was obviously hurt and wounded because of the things she recently had to walk through. Yet in all the tension of that moment, I sensed I was talking to a warrior. Wounded for sure, but a man of unique capabilities and potential.

He was the only man who had the courage to step forward in his district to seek help. My wife and I had talked to more than four hundred pastors and leaders in their district, sharing with them how they could get help with their sexual struggles and they would not be fired in the process. Since our research has revealed that more than fifty percent of pastors struggle with some sort of sexual bondage, there should have been fifty other pastors sitting with him. But, alas, such is the level of denial in the church. Nick asked me if anyone else had signed up to seek help. I smiled and said, "Nope. I guess you are the sacrificial lamb. They are waiting to see what we do to you before they risk stepping forward!"

Nick and his wife courageously walked through the healing process with many tears, copious amounts of laughter, and valiant hearts that I grew to respect deeply. They became leaders in their denomination with an escalation of honesty and integrity concerning sexual bondage. Nick is an anointed and creative servant leader whom I deeply respect. This book is not just a testimonial. It is far more than that. It is an emotional guidebook for your heart to grow in courage and purity. Personal application of the exercises and tools included in this book will help you to understand yourself much better and come to grips with why you do what you do.

I recommend that you read Nick's book with an open heart because he has a delightful way with words and is a creative thinker. My first impression of Nick was spot on as the Holy Spirit spoke to my soul. Nick is a warrior with a uniquely passionate heart for God! His words will stir your heart and give courage to your soul no matter what you may be battling!

Dr. Ted Roberts, President
Pure Desire Ministries Int'l.

INTRODUCTION

The Spirit of the LORD *is upon me, for he has anointed me to bring Good News to the poor. He has sent me to proclaim that captives will be released, that the blind will see, that the oppressed will be set free, and that the time of the Lord's favor has come.* Jesus, quoting Isaiah the prophet in Luke 4:18-19

Have you ever felt like your faith isn't working? Oh, I know we're not supposed to think of faith in pragmatic terms like success or failure, working or not, but let's be real. We have to talk about it. Sooner or later, the things we believe must either "work" in our lives or we will abandon them as powerless. We follow Jesus, not just because His words are intellectually and historically true, but because His words bring peace, joy, and life itself. Or at least that is the hope. So what do we do when His words, and our faith, aren't working?

For much of my life, I tried to hide the fact that some things I believed really did not work. I could see promise after promise that Jesus made in Scripture, but when I looked at my life, I could not see the evidence of His promises coming true. Rather than stopping and questioning this problem, I chose to put my head down and believe harder, hoping that sooner or later what Jesus promised would actually become my real life experience.

One promise in particular that always bugged me was John 8:32 where Jesus declares that His followers will "know the truth, and the truth shall set you free." I felt deep in my heart that I "knew the truth." I had met Jesus as a young boy and never really turned away from Him. I grew up the son of a preacher man who was the son of a preacher man. How much more truth could you need than knowing Jesus and hearing His words weekly from your own father, and his father before him? But I was not free.

For more than sixteen years of my life, I was addicted to pornography. For ten of those years, I was also a pastor. These two ideas are not supposed to go together. Pastor and porn; just putting the two words so close feels somehow defiling. The pastor is the spiritual leader, the one who has it all together. The pastor searches God's Word and then brings out the depths and riches of God's truth, having, of course, applied it to his own life first. I felt, however, like the spiritual cripple struggling to keep my faith together. I could really pull it off on the outside, though. If you ever sat in my church, you would certainly have been convinced that I knew the truth!

But every so often I would run across that verse and a pain would twinge in my heart. The mocking voice in my mind would grumble, *Really, Jesus? Knowing your truth will set me free? How I wish it were true!* The truth that I did know was that pornography was wrecking my life. On February 16, 2010, I was on the verge of losing my marriage, and with it my ministry.

Freedom felt like a far cry from what I was experiencing. I had a great wife. We met in college and fit perfectly together. Plus, she was way out of my league and I knew it from day one. We had three beautiful children, each one healthy, smart, and fully alive. I had an active, growing church filled with good people who genuinely seemed to like one another and appreciate me as their pastor. I had a good reputation and lots of latitude to try out my ideas and implement vision. All of this and I was only thirty-two years old, already enjoying the life only dreamt of by some others in my profession. But none of this seemed to matter in the secret place of my soul. I was about to lose it all because when it came to lust and purity, I always seemed to choose on the wrong side. And because of that, I was on the brink of destruction.

But this is not the sad story of how it all disappeared and God pulled me from the ashes of my own funeral pyre. This is the story of how God saved me from myself before it was too late. This is the story of how I discovered that Jesus' promise was actually true. And I believe it is true for you, too. Whether you are a pastor or a poet, a teacher or a techie, a logger or a learner, Jesus has promised to set you free.

COMMON GROUND

My guess is that on some level, we have all been here. We are frequent visitors to the place where what we believe doesn't match up with how we behave. The belief doesn't even have to be biblical per se, but just an ideal of how to live well. When our inability to live out these ideals is a "once in awhile" kind of event, we can chalk it up to a lack of discipline or a lapse of judgment. But when these slips become an ongoing part of our routine, we instinctively know something is wrong at a deep level. We know the right thing to do, but for whatever reason we fail to do it. This is a miserable place, is it not? But I think if we are willing to be honest, which I want to encourage you to do throughout this book, we can all see this place in ourselves.

There's the guy who has a great wife, great kids and a great job, but still he seeks out pleasure through the Internet or magazines. For other men, it goes further—to strip clubs, prostitutes, or through multiple affairs. These men are not alone.

There's also the guy who knows the family is on a tight budget, and each dollar must be accounted for in order to put food on the table and keep the creditors from calling. And yet he finds himself pulling again into the casino parking lot or logging on to the Internet poker room.

There's the gal who knows her weight and eating habits are a problem, maybe even causing some health concerns. But late at night she finds herself sitting on the couch with a bag of chips or Oreo cookies disappearing one by one.

There's the newly married man who really loves his wife and wants to put her first, but time and time again he finds himself in front of a football game, or holding a controller and achieving the next level, or heading out to drink with his buddies. The look on her face makes him promise himself this will be the last time, but somehow it never is.

There's the young mom who wants to raise her little kids well and teach them patience, kindness, and love. But inevitably the days get long, the chores pile up, and she finds herself giving way to anger, losing her temper and saying things she promised she would never say to her kids.

There's the couple that think they'll be married soon and they truly want a godly marriage, but the lure of hooking up and sleeping together seems to be too powerful a desire to resist. They want to believe it's all innocent and okay because they'll make it official soon enough, but something in their hearts protest that they are doing unforeseen damage to their future.

I could go on. So could you. But, hopefully, this is more than enough for all of us to pause and say, "We are all in this boat together, aren't we?" We know the right thing to do, whether that idea of right comes from the Bible, our family of origin, or just a personal sense of morality. We know it, but we don't do it.

Surprisingly, this idea surfaces in Scripture. The apostle Paul, one of the early leaders in the church and the greatest missionary of all time, wrote, "I don't understand myself, for I want to do what is right, but I don't do it. Instead, I do the very thing I hate" (Romans 7:15). You try to go to church. Paul started the church. You try to read your Bible. Paul wrote your Bible. And yet he is the one saying these very words that we could echo with a hearty, "Amen." Is there hope in this human predicament? I think so.

JESUS AND FREEDOM

I have no doubt that Jesus arrived on the scene and promised people freedom. Jesus' first recorded public words, according to the Bible account in Luke 4:18-19, are to quote Isaiah 61: "The Spirit of the Lord is upon me, for he has anointed me to bring Good News to the poor. He has sent me to proclaim that captives will be released, that the blind will see, that the oppressed will be set free, and that the time of the Lord's favor has come." When Jesus was done reading these words in that first-century Jewish synagogue, he did something unthinkable. He rolled up the scroll and said, "These words just came true today!" Jesus proclaimed that he was the fulfillment of those words. And you know what? He was. The rest of the book of Luke is a page-by-page description of blind people seeing, lame people walking, dead people rising, and captives of all sorts being delivered. When Jesus said those words, He actually meant for them to happen in a physical, tangible way.

If Jesus promised freedom and delivered freedom in His day, why is it that so few of us are truly feeling free and living free? We are forced to make one of several assumptions because of this. We either have to assume 1) these promises were a metaphor for spiritual, eternal freedom (which is clearly *not* what Jesus had in mind when He spoke them); 2) Jesus was lying; or 3) there is something wrong with us. Either we don't get it and don't know how to experience freedom, or we are too sinful, evil, mean, dirty, and we aren't good enough. Most Christians immediately dismiss option two and land on either one or three, and both conclusions are unfortunate. Choosing door number one reduces most of our faith down to propositional truth, ideas that we believe to be true, but don't really expect to experience in the here and now. "Heaven will be great," we say, "so just do your best and hold on to God's grace until then." We minimize our earthly experience to a sort of half-life where we are still losing the battle to sin and evil desires even though God has won the war in an eternal way.

Choosing door number three isn't much better. Here we assume that Jesus can be trusted and that He really did mean for us to experience those promises in this life. So, the reality that we are not experiencing them means that our faith is somehow deficient. We look around and feel like everyone else (well, most others at least) has it figured out. They seem "free" in our estimation, but we look in our own hearts and know that we are not. This results in a "try harder" approach to faith. Because everyone else seems to have it figured out, we keep quiet for the most part and redouble our efforts to be better. Or, others may simply choose to give up, deciding that their faith really doesn't work.

Could there be another option? Door number four? Could it possibly be that Jesus meant what He said in a real and practical way, He wasn't lying, and we are not spiritually inept? What if the issue is that we haven't fully understood *how* Jesus sets us free? What if the question isn't whether or not He can or does set us free, but what if our primary need is to understand the way in which that freedom comes? That would be an attractive option to me. That might cause me to open up my heart a little and say, "Jesus, show me this way!" I hope it might do the same for you, because that's what this book is all about. This is the journey that I have taken to real freedom. And the journey was much different than I expected it would be.

"This is the one thing we could never talk about in church."

While I believe this book will have practical application for people in all walks of life struggling with all kinds of behavior, the foundational story is our struggle with sexual sin. The Bible alerts us that sexual sin *is* somehow different. It strikes our hearts and our minds in a unique way: "No other sin so clearly affects the body as this one does. For sexual immorality is a sin against your own body" (1 Corinthians 6:18). I think that we instinctively know this because it somehow feels different. We may not be able to fully explain the how or the why, but it makes sexual sin particularly difficult to address.

Over the last two years, I have listened to a number of men share their stories of addiction, pain, frustration, and loss. One of the common statements they make is, "This is the one thing we could never talk about in church." Isn't that the truth? Oh sure, addressing weakness and sin of any kind can be a tough swallow in a church crowd, but start talking about sexual sin and see what happens. Eyes dart away nervously; mothers scan the room to see if innocent children need to be shooed out; people shuffle anxiously in their seats. We know this is different because it feels different.

Additionally, there is the reality that this may be the one addiction where society doesn't back us up. Have an issue with alcohol? We've got a class for you, society says, and we'll help you get through this. Have a gambling addiction? Here's a hotline you can call and get the help you need. But to struggle with sexual issues is unique. On the one hand, most sexual behaviors will be dismissed as normal "guy stuff," sowing our wild oats, or just a basic human urge. Who can resist, right? But on the other hand, if our sexual behavior has led us into anything deviant or illegal, which it often does, we get labeled as a pervert, an offender, or a sicko. Either direction seems like a real dead end.

This is why I am absolutely convinced that addressing human sexuality is *the* great challenge of our time. If people of faith and communities of faith can't learn how to wrestle with God's truth and our desires, then our sex-crazed culture will flatten our hearts with a ten-ton steamroller. It doesn't have to be this way. God has a plan for each and every one of us, and that plan includes true freedom in our sexuality. He has a gift He wants to give us, but learning to receive it may be more of a journey than we expect.

MY APPROACH TO WRITING THIS BOOK

Every author writes with a certain slant to his or her book. The writer sits in a certain chair that gives some unique insight into writing. A few of these chairs may be:

THE EXPERT'S CHAIR

The experts have all the answers because it is their field of expertise. They have read widely and studied the topic meticulously. They have conducted untold numbers of surveys and interviewed countless subjects to arrive at common threads that will change us all. They are the doctors and professors among us. While I have studied a bit and done what I can to understand the field of human sexuality, I am not primarily an expert. There are experts among us, and I would highly recommend you read their findings.

THE TESTIMONIAL CHAIR

This is the person whose life story is so powerful that you simply can't turn away. The script of the author's life is like a movie that won't let you go. We read these stories because the writer has lived and experienced the truth of his or her words on a super-sized platter. I will certainly be sharing my story with you, but I want to acknowledge up front here that my story is, I believe, very common. I believe our stories may have much in common. But I also realize that my story may not compare to the drama, loss, intensity or proportion of yours. And that's okay. Because I believe that underneath it all, we are having a common experience.

THE TRENDY CHAIR

This is the person who sits on the cutting edge of everything—technology, the Internet, cell phones, literature, you name it. They write about things you haven't even heard of yet. They analyze trends and ideas that are coming up in order to prepare us for what's next. While I believe that addressing sexual bondage is as current and relevant as anything in the world, I am not trendy. I don't know the latest or greatest thing going on. But I do see what's happening in the world around me and within me when it comes to human sexuality, and I think something needs to be said about it.

THE PASTOR'S CHAIR

I want to be honest to say that the chair I sit in is primarily the **Pastor's Chair**. I may not be an aged, seasoned veteran of the craft, but I have been a pastor at heart for as long as I can remember. As I mentioned before, I am a third generation pastor and I have spent my whole life in the church. I would like to tell you about a radical time of rebellion because I know it would be a gripping story, but I just never did that. I tried from day one to do what was right, and occasionally succeeded. My life experience has taken me through literally hundreds of churches, dozens of Christian schools, and numerous pastoral gatherings. I know the pastor and I know the pulpit and I know the pew (or new padded chairs that conveniently hook together) about as well as anyone. I know the good, the bad, and the ugly.

I say all of this to tell you that throughout the book, my approach will be to share what I see as the interaction between life, human sexuality, and God's Word. Rather than looking at research or surveys (though I will reference some), I will turn primarily to the Bible and ask the question, "How does God see this? How did God intend for this to work?" I think this view is increasingly significant in a world which seems to have forgotten that God has a better way for us.

I will also be turning regularly toward the church in order to ask, "How can churches become the kind of healing place God meant us to be?" I don't know about you, but I am getting so sick of "church nice" that I'm thinking of putting it in our title. You know what I mean, right? (Welcome to the Church of You Don't Have to Pretend You're Fine. Long title, but it says something!) We come to church broken, confused, frustrated, and feeling alone. We walk in and someone says, "Hey brother! How are you?" And we respond, "Great. Fine. Doing fine. Everything's good. Just fine as fine can be!" We say this because we think we're supposed to. And we believe that everyone else really is fine and their lives are nice. So rather than stick out, we play church nice. And then we go home broken, confused, frustrated, and feeling alone. This is not what Jesus had in mind when He told Peter that He was building His church. Jesus envisioned a gathering of all kinds of people—broken, religious, irreligious, rebellious, afraid, you name it—who would be united by one thing and one thing alone: Jesus. Being "fine" or having it all together does not make us the church. Jesus does. And when He builds the church, authenticity and freedom have a chance.

THE CHIASTIC STRUCTURE OF THE BOOK

I apologize for the intimidating, academic feel of that word. I know "chiastic" isn't a word you pull out very often. ("Hey guys, have you noticed how completely chiastic my golf game is today?") Simply put, the word "chiastic" means that the most important idea is in the middle, and everything that leads up to it roughly parallels everything that trails away. So, if I say three things to you in a "chiastic" manner, sentences one and three will match up, and sentence two in the middle will be the main idea. If you look at the table of contents again, you'll even see visually how this is set up.

Why use this literary method? For starters, this is one of the most common approaches used in Scripture. We see chiasms throughout the Psalms, prophets, and in Jesus' stories. One author I know of believes the whole book of Revelation should be seen as chiastic. To be honest, I'm not really sure why they did this in the Bible, but at least you know now that it's not a new idea.

My idea of the chiasm is to acknowledge that the most important ideas of this book are probably in the middle, around the time that God really showed up in my life and set me on a path of freedom away from pornography. The ideas and concepts that have meant the most to me were all birthed in this time. But please don't skip ahead and just read the middle! There is a path to take toward this breakthrough moment. I am calling the first five chapters "The Addictive Path." Our story of getting hooked into sexual sin started much earlier than we want to believe; seeing the first steps can make all the difference. And the path itself is the set-up for understanding the moment of transformation and the subsequent healing. If we simply look for breakthrough without understanding the path that leads to it, breakthrough will not occur. So go with me to the beginning, because God will meet us at the trailhead.

Chapter 6 is the "Breakthrough Peak," but after this the story isn't over. This is one of the fallacies we believe about recovery—that we need this moment of freedom so that we can move on. I believe freedom starts in a moment, but it is ultimately a journey. To arrive at a breakthrough point and not proceed onward sets us up to slide back down the addictive path. Freedom is a process of all the old places being transformed into new ones. You will see in the chiastic structure how God makes all things new from birth to adolescence to marital intimacy. I will call this path that moves forward from the peak "The Healing Path" (Chapters 7 through 11). Now you know how to understand the structure of this book. You also know a catchy sentence to pull out on your next golf outing.

ENTERING THE BOOK

I believe that's all you need to know to enter into this book. Can I just say how completely honored and humbled I am that you are choosing to do so? I know from experience, this is an area of life that is easier to avoid than address. But my guess, if I know you like I know myself, is that something in your brain is crying out to say, *There has to be a better way than all of this!* I hope this book might be God's reply to your declaration. You can be free!

PART 1: THE ADDICTIVE PATH

CHAPTER ONE | BIRTH

Wait. We can't start a book about sexual addiction by talking about babies. Babies are innocent and pure. To even speak of them in the same sentence as our struggle with human sexuality seems to violate the universal human belief in innocence.

Babies themselves are innocent, yes. I've been in the room for the birth of four of my own now, and there is a beauty, honesty, and innocence in the moment of their arrival that cannot be described in words alone. Babies may be innocent, but our birth stories and birth environments never are; they are fraught with pain, brokenness, dysfunction, and sin. You see, babies are born into the real world; the last time I checked, this world can be a pretty rough place. Here's the real problem, though: Because we see babies as innocent, we rarely look back that far for clues about what's going on in our life. We assume that all our problems began much later when we had the power to choose and we could decide between right and wrong. It may be true that our *active participation* in wrongdoing began later, but the seeds of these behaviors were planted at birth. These clues are essential to our story.

MY STORY: OH GIVE ME A HOME

One of the realities we need to address is that we have no choice over when and where we are born, or to whom. All of these are "chosen" for us, whether we think God actively does this or it's just random fate and probability. Either way, the choice was completely out of our hands. So in speaking of our birth, we can be rational and fair. We don't need to defend or blame what happened so much as we need to understand the power it had in shaping us.

My story began in the rural Wyoming town of Greybull, population 1,500. This town sprang up along the railroad as a stop for the buying and selling of cattle and grain. One hundred years later, about all that kept it alive was its proximity to Yellowstone National Park's eastern entrance near Cody. Greybull was not, and is not, a destination kind of place. I can't tell you how many people have said to me that they "stayed in Greybull" once. It had cheap motels and lots of empty rooms. But I can't remember a single person telling me they ever "went to Greybull."

While it may not have been a huge destination city, Greybull is a nice place to be from. I was born second oldest in a family of four children. You would think my parents planned it: girl, boy, girl, boy, evenly spaced by about a year and a half each. My mom will quickly tell you that this was not the case; it just happened that way. What this meant, though, is that we were within four and one-half years of each other from oldest to youngest. We were close in birth, close through school, and close in just about every life experience.

My dad was a pastor and led a small Christian and Missionary Alliance church that sat right beside the main road through town. When he and mom first arrived, the church had about twenty saints keeping the doors open. As a young and ambitious twenty-something, my dad built the church both numerically and physically. By the time I was old enough to remember, the church was a nice group of eighty people meeting weekly to sing hymns and hear Dad preach the Word.

My mom worked as a nurse at the local hospital, starting in labor and delivery and then moving to the nursing care side of the operation. With small children at home, I think she preferred the pace of those folks to the sporadic intensity of childbirth. To this day, I couldn't tell you who earned more—Mom or Dad— but I would guess neither income alone provided quite enough for our family of six. We grew up lower middle class, as most did in Greybull, without much money to spare.

So why take the time to tell you all of this? These details must seem trivial compared to the real matter at hand. Not so! You see, hidden within my rather bland, if not idyllic, description of childhood are some key factors that have been at play in my life ever since. For starters, I think being tight on money as a family stuck with me and even contributed to a need in my life for control and safety. Plus, this economic pressure forced my mom to work outside the home, which added to the general stress level in our family. But these factors pale in comparison to the main one; in looking back on my life, I would say I was set up for a lifetime of attention-grabbing behavior. "Notice me" became my theme. Both my mom and dad were in the middle of many activities and very busy, and their attention had to be divided among my three siblings and me. I was a middle child. I was from a small town in the middle of nowhere. All of this led to performance-driven behaviors; I wanted to be noticed by someone and get out of the middle behaviors, both good and bad!

I can almost hear the skeptic inside of you pushing back to this notion: "Really? C'mon! You can't see all those behaviors just from your birth scenario." Maybe, maybe not. But I would say, I can see all the beginnings of these behaviors that have been woven into my life ever since. If I fail to see where they started, I will be powerless to change them.

Our birth story and situation is a reality that we must accept. How many people spend their lives trying to run away or ignore where they began? The country girl can move to the big city, but the country has and will forever shape her. The rich kid can join the Peace Corps and head to Africa, but his upbringing will continue to shape him unless he recognizes its impact. The question is not whether or not our birth has affected us. The real question is whether or not we will be attentive to *how* it has shaped us. Let's look at a rather stark example of where this shows up in Scripture.

GOD'S STORY: HE WAS THERE

While some may argue over whether our birth was the natural outcome of free will or the exact choosing of God's providence, Scripture makes it clear that God was there from the beginning. In one of the most moving songs in the Bible we read, "You made all the delicate, inner parts of my body and knit me together in my mother's womb…You watched me as I was being formed in utter seclusion, as I was woven together in the dark of the womb. You saw me before I was born. Every day of my life was recorded in your book. Every moment was laid out before a single day had passed! How precious are your thoughts about me, O God!" (Psalm 139: 13, 15-17). This means that even before we were born, God was already encoding Himself and His plans into our heart, mind and soul. We are His craftsmanship and we must never forget this!

Since we are His creation, our value and His esteem for us were secured at the very moment of our birth. Nothing we ever say or do could make Him love us less. We can't perform our way into His love, and we can't "un-perform" our way out of it!

I know this because I see it in the Bible and because I have experienced it. And you have also experienced it, if you have ever had children. Think back to the moment when your son or your daughter first opened their little eyes to this big, bright world. What were you feeling in your heart? Perhaps you, like me, felt an overwhelming rush of love. All at once, a piece of your heart was forever tied up in that little, pinkish eight and a half pound baby. And you knew, in that moment, nothing that child ever said or did could change the way you felt. Oh sure, they could break your heart a million times, drive you crazy with their questions, or keep you up all hours of the night with worry. But stop loving them? Not a chance. Think of them as worthless or useless? Never. And if we, as imperfect, human dads and moms can feel these emotions, how much more does God's heart beat for us? How much more does the perfect Heavenly Father care for you?

We must never forget this, because while God was shaping us, evil was at work in the world. From day one, it has been a competition to see which voice would win out as the loudest. A compelling example of this in Scripture is the man Gideon. When we first meet Gideon in the book of Judges, it is obvious which side has been winning. For starters, Gideon's life occurred during a dark time in Israel's history. This was a time when Israel had no king and people "did whatever seemed right in their own eyes" (Judges 21:25). What's more, because the nation had defiled itself by worshipping false gods, the true God Jehovah had turned them over to be ruled by invading nations. In Gideon's lifetime, the Midianites, a wicked and cruel people, controlled the land.

The Midianites were so oppressive and harsh that Gideon is preparing grain in a wine press (Judges 6). This would most likely have been a cave, a place of hiding, where Gideon cowered as he worked the grain, knowing that if he was seen by the Midianites, his grain would be taken. It is to this poor, unfortunate soul that an angel of the Lord appears and shouts, "Mighty Hero! The Lord is with you." God sees something in Gideon that Gideon cannot see in himself. God has made him and chosen him to be mighty! How great is that?

Gideon's response, though, is pretty funny. He completely ignores the "mighty hero" part and jumps right to "the Lord is with you" comment. Gideon's reply, in my own words, is to say, "Oh really? If God is with us, then why is life so rotten? I heard as a boy that God delivered our people from Egypt, but here we are being oppressed by an inferior nation. No, my winged friend, God is not with us." Gideon's birth situation had predisposed him to doubt God's presence and protection.

But the angel goes on undeterred: "Go with the strength you have and rescue Israel from the Midianites. I am sending you!" Now the angel is being funny. Here's a wimpy kid hiding out and preparing the grain (a woman's job in that hierarchical society) and the angel tells him to go in the strength he has. What strength? But God is declaring to Gideon, "What I gave you at birth is enough to accomplish what I will give you in life. I am sending you and I am with you, and I made you to be mighty!"

Gideon, however, only picks up on the irony of the statement. Again in my words, he says, "Yeah right! You are talking to the littlest guy in the weakest family in a very average tribe. What can I possibly do?" I think from day one, Gideon has interpreted from his circumstance, his birth order, and the position of his family in the tribe that he is a weakling. A real nobody. Certainly, Gideon grew into this mindset, but can you see how it was all encoded into his thinking from the beginning?

To make a long story short, Gideon's winged friend finally convinces him that God truly is with him (remember the whole wet fleece, dry ground thing? That's Gideon). Then God gathers an army that quickly gets whittled down to a mere three hundred men. This merry band of warriors goes out with little more than lanterns and trumpets and surrounds an army that appeared as large as a "swarm of locusts" and their camels too many to count! (Judges 7:12). At Gideon's command, the lanterns all light up, the trumpets sound, and in a mad dash of panic the enemy completely annihilates itself.

What a proud moment for Israel, and for Gideon. I have heard this message preached dozens of times. But I have rarely heard the rest of the story. Have you? Gideon's story begins well and seems to be a real rags-to-riches thriller where the nobody becomes a somebody and directs all the people back to God. Gideon starts there, but sadly he doesn't end there.

You see, Gideon's first words to the army proclaim that God has given them victory (Judges 7:15); later he has the army shout, "For the Lord *and* for Gideon!" (Judges 7:18, italics mine), and by the end of his life, the people are saying, "Gideon has rescued us" (Judges 8:22). In fact, in the final chapter of Gideon's life, he asks the people to make him a special priestly garment. This kind of robe was originally given to Aaron, the brother of Moses who was the first high priest over Israel. Attached to the garment (called an ephod) was a breastplate that Aaron and the subsequent high priests wore into the Presence of God as representatives of Israel's twelve tribes. Only the high priest, a Levite, was to wear the ephod as a sign of his holy standing before God.

So what on earth is Gideon doing? He's taking worship that belonged to God and receiving it himself. In speaking of this event, Judges 8:27 says, "Soon all the Israelites prostituted themselves by worshiping it [the ephod], and it became a trap for Gideon and his family." At the beginning of his life, he had the people cheering, "Yeah, God!" But by the end, he had them all chanting, "Yeah, Gideon." Which is ironic, because absolutely everything God did through Gideon was intentionally designed to show that no human being could possibly have pulled off this story; God alone should get the glory for what had happened. Yet each chapter of Gideon's life is a sad slide from "Yeah, God!" to "Yeah, me." As the years passed, the work of God became less and less important, and the praise for self mattered more and more to Gideon. Why? Gideon never left his birthplace and he never truly left the winepress. Even though God did astounding things through him, Gideon was still fighting the pernicious voice in his head that said, "You're a weakling. You're nobody. You were born into a weak clan and you're still the weakest one."

What do you do if you are the least? You spend your life trying to prove that you are the best; when Gideon had the opportunity, that's exactly what he did. I wonder if Gideon ever realized that the battle he was fighting, and losing, was this battle. Gideon's life could have counted for so much more, but when he died, the people of Israel immediately fell back into worshipping false gods. This is what Gideon taught them to do when he made the ephod. His inability to alter the messages of his birth story would alter the future of a whole generation by turning them away from God and into sin.

OUR STORY: NOT AVOIDING, BUT UNDERSTANDING

Believe it or not, you and I have a great deal in common with Gideon. As with his birth, so also our birth story and circumstance have had a profound impact on how we see ourselves and how we function to this very day. But God also sees something in us that we cannot see. God knows what He has put in us and what can be called out of us. And, like Gideon, the choice we make concerning which voice will be the loudest has tremendous bearing on the legacy we leave behind. People will be influenced through us; there is no doubt about that. What hangs in the balance is whether our influence will have more to do with the negative voices of our past or the life-giving voice of God's Spirit.

Some of you, particularly if your early environment was negative or abusive, will have a strong desire to ignore or avoid this part of your life. It seems better to move on and focus on other, more positive, life experiences. We believe that if we think about a negative beginning, we open ourselves up to the emotion of it all and give those memories power over us.

Consider, though, that the exact opposite may be occurring; that in trying to ignore or avoid the troubling pieces of your past, you are actually giving them great power over you. Author Anthony de Mello, in his insightful book, *Awareness*, says, "When you fight something, you're tied to it forever. As long as you're fighting it, you are giving it power. You give it as much power as you are using to fight it."[1] When you try to ignore or avoid your past, you are fighting against it; this gives your past power in your life. Your birth story or painful experiences along the way become the giant elephant in the room that continues to define you.

How, exactly, do we remove the power the past can have over our lives? How do we empty that voice of its control and diminish the volume? As de Mello says, not by "renouncing it, but by seeing through it and understanding its true value."[2] What we need is the ability to tell our life story as a coherent narrative. This means that we can piece together our past and present in a sensible way. Like a jigsaw puzzle, we start placing together all of the seemingly random moments and experiences into one grand picture of the person we are. When we can see and understand how the pieces fit together, individual pieces, whether our birth story or something later in life, lose their power over us. We can begin to hear the voice of God and see His plan, even through places of pain.

In his landmark workbook on sexual addiction, Dr. Ted Roberts reports on a study done by Dr. Mary Main called the Adult Attachment Interview.[3] This study set out to understand why some children had a healthy sense of attachment or security in their lives while others did not. The interviewers asked parents a set of questions about their childhood in an attempt to determine how well they could make sense of their own upbringing.

Here's what they discovered (quoting Roberts): "If the parent could share a coherent, reflective and emotionally engaged narrative about their childhood, the more likely it was the children would have a good relationship with them. It didn't matter how inadequate or abusive the parent's family of origin may have been. It didn't matter what may have happened to them. *The determining factor was how they made sense out of what happened to them.*"

The implications of this for you and me are huge! This means that our background has far less power than we think; it is our ability to make sense of our background that matters most. As Roberts says, "If you can make sense of your story, you can change its impact on your life."

For me, I had always assumed I was just a performer. I liked to be on a stage and to be noticed. I loved applause and admiration. This seemed to be nothing more than a matter of how I was wired. But over the last few years, I have been able to look back at my story and see that performance is far more than something I do. Performance has become a way that I define myself, a way of determining if I am okay or not. Since day one, I needed to be noticed and performance became the most successful route. I haven't quit performing. I still stand on a stage regularly to preach and do many things that are "in the public eye." But my mind is shifting. I don't need these things to define myself like I used to. I am finding greater freedom in now performing for His glory. And this somehow feels more like God's dream and calling than my own.

Here are some other examples of how a birth story becomes a false identity. See if any of them trigger a deeper understanding of what you may have acquired:

- The child born into a wealthy home where every convenience is to be had and life is a continual experience of new and better things. This person will wrestle with feelings of entitlement and a continual need for things in life to be better, bigger, and more exciting or else they get bored.

- The only child who is doted upon from day one. They rarely go without and they become accustomed to the spotlight and attention. This person could struggle with feeling that life owes them and that their needs should always be the priority of others.

- The oldest child who feels pressure to perform. As first-born, some oldest children grow up carrying the mantle of the family. They were the first out of the womb, and so received all of the parents' well-studied efforts at childrearing, as well as all of the parents early mistakes. This individual might live with a high-level of anxiety over measuring up in life and might also feel the need to hold themselves and others to a perfectionist standard.

- The youngest child who has to act up in order to be noticed. Born last among many, the youngest child is often the pride and joy of the family. But older siblings have all the events, school activities, and drama that steal away the attention. This individual could be the class clown and the constant comedian to get people's attention.

- The child born in a broken, unstable home. From day one, this person has known instability, chaos, and mobility, often living in several places during the first five years of life. As an adult, they may wrestle with significant issues of trust, and either the extreme desires of moving every few years or never moving out of fear of change.

These are just a few, general examples to get you going. The million-dollar question, though, is: Can you make sense of your story? Can you see through it and understand it, or are you blind to the influence it has over you even to this day? What about your birth story has "identified" you? Like Gideon, have you embraced some negative ideas that are louder and stronger than even the voice of God in your life?

Here are three suggestions about how you might work on telling a coherent narrative of your life and determining the impact your past has had on you:

1) THE STORYBOARD

Grab a pad of sticky notes and sit at an empty table or with a large poster board in a quiet place. This activity is helpful for the more spatial, creative types. Begin thinking through your life in stages: birth, early childhood, grade school, adolescence, college, and beyond. On each sticky note, write down the significant people, memories, experiences, victories, and sorrows; write only one idea per sticky note. Fill up as many notes as you need for each life stage. When you have done this for each stage, sit back and read through them. Look for patterns and overlap that will emerge as themes of your life. Start to place sticky notes together in clusters around these themes. This can be a particularly powerful experience with a mentor or a small group of trusted friends.

2) THE AUTOBIOGRAPHY

If you tend to be a more linear, point-to-point thinker, this method might work better. Take time to write a rough draft of your life story. Don't worry about length—four or five pages would probably do it—but tell the story of your life like a movie script or television drama. Try not to control the outcome or direction of the story, but simply start at the beginning and write the drama as you remember it. When you're finished, read it and look for connections that run beginning to end. Again, this can be particularly helpful to do with someone who knows you well and can see what you cannot see.

3) THE COFFEE TALK

Take some casual time with a friend (a casual acquaintance might be better) over a cup of coffee (or tea, or beer, or soda, or whatever you like to drink) and rehearse the details of your life. It might be best to tell it as a hypothetical story or a case study. (Let's say that a boy named Rick was born in a rural town in Wyoming...) Bring out as many details of your birth story and circumstances as you can remember. When you have finished—and this is the key moment—ask your friend, "What do you think someone with this birth story would likely struggle with in life? What fertile soil do you see for this person to allow lies and deception into their life about who they are?" I will bet that 90-95% of the time, your friend will nail it. Why? Because others can see from the outside what we fail to see from within. We have become so familiar with the voices, the lies that run our life, that they can become background music we no longer hear. A friend's ears will pick up on the out-of-tune rhythms and graciously open our ears as well.

UM...I THOUGHT THIS BOOK WAS ABOUT SEXUAL ADDICTION?

Why start here, you may ask? That's a fair question, because I haven't even mentioned porn, sex, or addiction in this chapter. What does birth have to do with our sexuality and addiction? Everything! We must be able to see our life story and the power it has over us. We must understand its true value and how it has shaped us. Until we do this, we are powerless to change it. I'm not talking about strange methods of psychotherapy or trying to recreate the past. I am talking about acknowledging that the time, place, and circumstance of our birth set into motion much of who we are today. When we see the effect all of this had on us, we can begin to reinterpret our life story.

You see, one of the great struggles in our sexual sin is self-blindness. We know *when* it has happened. We know exactly *what* we did that made us feel bad, shameful, dirty, sinful, or unclean before God and others. Our actions speak loudly and because of this we tend to focus on them. And most methods of recovery and change focus on changing these obvious behaviors. Such methods are doomed to fail, at times leaving us more discouraged than when we began.

Freedom is the result, not of knowing *what* we did and changing it, but of knowing *why* we do what we do. We know what. The what is easy. Understanding why is the key to change. Here's the truth about sexual sin: Sexual sin is *never* the simplistic acting out of our fleshly desires. You may have been told this, but it is a lie! Our physical, human desires are certainly part of the equation, but only part. The reason we give in to and follow these desires is *always* because something else is at work deeper in our heart and in our brain, most noticeably so when what we do contradicts what we believe. We violate our conscience, not merely because the human urge is too great, but because our life story has created a vacuum of need that our sexuality fills up. Don't worry if you're skeptical of this concept right now; I was for a long time, too. We'll come back to it often in subsequent chapters.

BUT I HAD GOOD PARENTS!

Particularly if we grew up in a relatively healthy or stable home, this kind of backtracking can be very difficult. We feel like doing so is looking for opportunities to blame our dad and mom for problems in our life. We love our parents and some of this may start to feel like betrayal.

But let me assure you, this is not the case. I am not trying to put anyone's folks, yours or mine, in a negative light. There is, however, the reality that your parents, like mine, were and are flawed human beings. They had weaknesses and shortcomings. They were not perfect. Like every person ever born, they were sinners. And this is the truth: *Our sin hurts others whether we want it to or not.* By the mere fact that they are human, your parents' sin had a negative effect on you. They may never have intended it to, and they may never have wanted it to. They may have loved you beyond any call of parental duty. But the fact remains: You were impacted by their imperfections. If we can admit this, it gives us freedom to look honestly at our past and determine how we are being affected by it today. We can also, then, invite God into those places of brokenness and allow Him to break generational curses. He can and does redeem all things for His glory.

THE LINCHPIN

One of the metaphors meaningful to me during this journey has been that of a caged bird. A caged bird has no less "birdness" to it than a free bird, but its life experience is very different from, and very contrary to, how God designed it. A caged bird is biologically a bird in shape, size, and appearance, but not in function. So also, when we are trapped in sexual sin, we are still human in form, but not in function. We were meant to be free and to fly. This means leaving the cage behind; and in order for that to happen, the door must open and we must fly out. I am choosing to call this critical moment—this moment when God's truth grabs our hearts and thrusts us out into the free air—the linchpin. The linchpin is used figuratively in language to describe anything that holds the various elements of a complicated structure together. (Thank you, Wikipedia, for that one!) Your sexual story is definitely a complicated structure. But we will discover chapter by chapter the crucial place where God's deliverance meets our brokenness. It is there that He will open the door to our cage and we must choose to fly.

The linchpin of our birth story is this: God shaped you and made you into somebody wonderful before you were ever born. But at birth, two voices began to simultaneously speak into your life: the loving voice of the Heavenly Father, and the deceptive voice of Satan in a fallen, broken world. Your identity has been radically shaped by one or the other, and in some ways, by both. The voice of God, and the revelation of His dreams and destiny for you, brings incredible freedom and joy. But the voice of Satan has been at work to cripple and demean you from day one. If you find yourself trapped in a behavior you can't seem to shake, it reveals the hold the enemy's voice has on your identity.

This is the moment of freedom where God opens the door to your cage. He comes along and speaks a new identity over you: mighty hero; man of honor; gifted musician for Me; beloved son or daughter. All of these titles and more could be appropriated to your life. But in our heads, like Gideon, we have another tune that has been playing for a long time. But this is it! This is the moment of decision. Which one will you believe? Which one will you tune in to and say, "This is my life frequency!"

This decision is what Colossians 3 talks about. This chapter reminds us beautifully that through Christ, we have been raised to new life and our real life is now hidden with Christ in God. With this truth in mind, we begin to "strip off" all of the old negative habits and patterns of the mind and the will. We put them to death, get rid of and have nothing to do with them. As we do, we then "put on" and clothe ourselves with our new nature: the mind and the habits of Christ. Off with the old, on with the new. Off with the old beliefs about who you are, what you'll amount to and what you're worth. On with the mind of Christ—His identity spoken over you and His dreams for you. It's time to fly!

Let the message about Christ, in all its richness, fill your lives. Teach and counsel each other with all the wisdom he gives. Sing psalms and hymns and spiritual songs to God with thankful hearts. Colossians 3:16

CHAPTER TWO | CHILDHOOD

Have you ever woke up in the morning and not been able to remember where you are? Okay, you could go in some pretty strange directions with that question, so let me explain. There was a time in college when I had been traveling quite a bit. I was on the school basketball team, and we routinely participated in weekend tournaments where we would stay the night in a hotel. In addition to this, I sang in a men's quartet that traveled from church to church doing concerts and recruiting for our school. It wasn't unusual for us to spend a night in two different host homes on a single weekend.

After about a month of these weekends, I woke up early on a Saturday morning and had this very unsettling feeling: I could not remember where I was. I had stayed in so many different places over the last month, and now the surroundings of the room I was in just weren't triggering anything in my brain. I lay there silently for a few minutes wondering what to do. As my mind started to put together the events from the day before, I finally had it. I was actually at my grandparents' house!

Now stick with me because I have a point here. I promise. My grandparents have lived in the same house since before I was born. I have been to their house dozens of times and slept in that very same bed on a number of occasions. Why, on this particular day, had I been unable to recognize a place that was so familiar to me? All of the travel from the previous month had served to disorient my brain. I had become so accustomed to waking up in unfamiliar rooms that when I finally woke up in one that was very familiar, my mind couldn't make sense of it.

Here's the point: Our brain can become easily disoriented. Childhood can be a very disorienting time. In our early years, we have a vast amount of new and different experiences, and our little brains are working overtime to keep it all pieced together in an orderly fashion. In this way, scientists tell us, our brains function a bit like a computer. Information and ideas get stashed in random places. The brain, like a computer hard drive, remembers the different pathways to access the information, but sometimes those pathways are very complex and non-linear.

All of this works out pretty well, until we experience something that violates our conscience. (The equivalent of a hard-drive crash!) At this point, we have a choice to make about how to process this new data. We can choose to talk about it with those we know and trust, and in this process of revelation make sense of what has happened. Or, we can choose to hide it. In order to hide it, we have to isolate from it. We have to become another person—one who is divided.

When I was a kid, I couldn't talk about sex. I am not sure when I learned this or how it was enforced in my psyche, but I somehow believed it was a topic that was taboo. Sex was very mysterious, adult-ish, and in some way dirty. Everything I knew about sex was either from the Bible, and the only parts I remember hearing talked about were what not to do, or from culture, not the greatest of teachers. Sex to me was basically sinful.

But I also knew somehow that married people had sex. So, I finally got the courage to ask my dad about this. The most awkward, wonderful, frightening, engaging conversation of my life occurred in the fourth grade when my dad and I had the proverbial "birds and the bees" talk. I can honestly say that I had never heard of such things before! The concepts that he described of the sexual interaction between a man and woman confounded and captured my mind and my imagination.

I remember going to school the next day and wondering if all the other kids knew what I knew. On one hand I felt tempted to ask all of my friends, "Hey, do you know what sex really is?" On the other hand I was petrified by this knowledge. I felt like the knowledge had awakened me to a whole new world, one for which I was only partially prepared, as is the case for every child. Sex, in ways innocent or not, enters our world before we are entirely ready. That is the only memory I have of ever discussing sex in my home as a child. We just didn't talk about that sort of thing in our home.

Around this time, I was old enough to start going to friends' houses alone. One such friend had an older brother in high school, and plastered around his walls were posters of girls sprawled out over Ferraris and Harleys, wearing an eye-patch worth of clothing. Something in me felt this was wrong, but we would just stand in his brother's room and look around for several minutes. When I went home, I was sure to never mention this part of the day.

At another friend's house, we would stay up after his parents had put us to bed and spy on the movies they were watching. We would creep quietly up the stairs and watch the "adult" movies they had picked. These weren't X-rated shows, but for a kid who had never seen anything R-rated, they might as well have been! I saw scenes depicted that created whole new caverns in my brain as it tried to comprehend what I was seeing. Once again, when I returned home, these events were never discussed.

On an even darker note, I had another friend who wanted us to "touch here, watch me do this, let me watch you do that." All of it made me feel gross. Somehow I knew this was a violation of my body and an affront to what God intended, but I liked this friend and I went along with it. I immediately and instinctively knew that this was something I could never tell my mom and dad. I knew they wouldn't like it and I would feel so embarrassed. I didn't want to be prohibited from playing and I didn't want to get my friend in trouble. So like all of the other events, I hid it. I kept it quiet and put it in the part of my brain that was now being created for such experiences.

At this age, I was too young to be aware of all these thoughts, but what began was a divide in my soul—a place where who I was needed to be hidden from public view because it was somehow abnormal and unacceptable. These stories were definitely not part of the hymn-singing, Bible-believing experience of the church I attended. I didn't know where else to process them, other than to stuff them deep inside and do my level best to keep acting like everybody else.

These experiences are sadly a part of childhood—exploring, learning, even being violated and not knowing what to say. Maybe your introduction into the world of human sexuality was harsher than mine. Maybe you were abused, or mistreated, or exposed to things that no child should have to see or experience. What we lack as a society is a healthy, family-based, faith-filled way to teach children about a godly form of sexuality, and so, in this absence, most of us learn through experience and from culture. Is it any wonder our world has become sexually out of control?

So what do we do? What do we do when our experiences can't be shared and leave us feeling somehow embarrassed and alone? We separate from it. We become dual citizens in our own body and mind. Our brain treats this as a traumatic event, and in order to keep us safe and sane, our brain files these experiences away in a place outside our normal processing, but still very much in view. So you learned perhaps, like I did, that this was an area of life you had to hide.

GOD'S STORY: WISDOM HAS ITS LIMITS

Where was God when all of this was happening to us? He was in the same place He has been since our first cells came together—right beside us and with us. "I know the LORD is always with me. I will not be shaken, for he is right beside me!" (Psalm 16:8). He was there, but as kids our concept of God is rather limited. I had a hard time separating my view of God from my view of my dad. The two, as I imagined at that time, were very similar except that God was bigger, stronger, more powerful, and harsher on misbehavior. If I had to hide these things from Dad, I definitely had to "hide" them from God!

Even as a kid, though, I knew this was impossible. I knew that God had seen everything I had done (and that had been done to me) and I couldn't help but think He was somehow displeased. If this was your feeling about God, know that you were not alone! How could the pure, righteous, holy God of eternity be pleased with me? And so this fear of having disappointed God actually reinforces the growing divide of self. As we try to hide the one side, we actively work on the good side, hoping that God will be pleased. We enter into a religious nightmare where nothing we do seems quite good enough because another reality is always lurking in the shadows.

What all of this produces in us is the ability to *believe* one way and *behave* another. As I mentioned in the introduction, this is common ground for us. We know the right thing to do, but we don't do it. Nowhere is this classic divide seen more clearly than in one of the wisest men to ever live, Solomon.

Solomon was the third king over all Israel. His father, David, had established a mighty kingdom and passed it on to Solomon during a time of peace. Early in his reign, Solomon found favor with God, so God granted him a request: anything he would like. Solomon chose wisdom to govern the people wisely. God was so pleased with this request that He gave Solomon not only the wisdom he requested, but riches and honor as well (1 Kings 3). Just like that, Solomon was the second wisest person the world has ever known. (I would still hold out that Jesus, the Son of God, had him beat!)

Now, you would expect that the second-wisest person to ever live would have life pretty well figured out, including his sexuality. If there was a person who would seem to have the mental capacity to choose what was right, it would be Solomon. And indeed, when it came to love, relationships, and women, Solomon had some pretty amazing and wonderful things to say. He put his wisdom to some good uses.

Take time and read *slowly* through Song of Songs and you'll hear the words of a man who understood love, passion, and longing. Read the wise advice of Proverbs, and you'll hear a man who knows how to avoid sexual temptation and honor the wife of his youth. Walk through the book of Ecclesiastes and you'll discover a man who could see through the emptiness and futility of carnal, fleshly pursuits. Solomon wrote all of these.

And yet, Solomon lived very differently than the way he wrote. Even though God had warned him against it, Solomon married often. Yes, it was common in those days for a king to have more than one wife, typically as a way to secure positive relationships with other kingdoms. But Solomon clearly goes beyond the call of the throne here. In 1 Kings 11, we read that Solomon had seven hundred wives. That's not a typo. That's a seven with two zeros. That's almost one wife a night for two years straight. But he didn't stop there; he also had in his possession (and I say possession intentionally) three hundred concubines. A concubine was essentially a young female available to the king sexually at moment's notice, but with no obligations of a marriage relationship. I don't think it's a stretch to call this three hundred "friends with benefits." Solomon was a busy guy, to say the least.

This is the same Solomon who actually wrote these words: "Drink water from your own well—share your love only with your wife...Let your wife be a fountain of blessing for you. Rejoice in the wife of your youth. She is a loving deer, a graceful doe. Let her breasts satisfy you always. May you always be captivated by her love" (Proverbs 5:15, 18-19). I don't see the use of the plural "wives" in here. I hear a very wise man instructing others to be devoted to one wife for a lifetime.

And yet Solomon couldn't do it. Not even close. So how does one of the wisest men ever fail to live out the value of his own words? I believe he had developed dual citizenship in his own body. I'm not talking about two different personalities, like someone with Dissociative Identity Disorder, but two sides to himself. Think about it this way (I am reading between the lines in Scripture here): Solomon's birth is the result of the most well-known illicit relationship of all time. David and Bathsheba's sin was public to the whole kingdom, and their first son had died as punishment for that sin (the Bible doesn't even give this child a name). Solomon grew up with this identity hanging over his life. Add to that a father who had multiple wives himself and was usually wrapped up in some political or military intrigue to protect the kingdom, and you have one messed-up kid left behind! How could Solomon not be a little warped in his soul from all this?

Also interesting is when Solomon asks God for wisdom (1 Kings 3:9): "Give me an understanding heart so that I can govern your people well and know the difference between right and wrong." Do you catch the subtle side of his request? He wants wisdom *for others*, so he can govern *them* well? In other words, he wants to be successful at his job, at what he does, but he doesn't ask God for wisdom to govern himself. He knew right and wrong, and his decisions and words are legendary. But his personal life was an absolute wreck.

Kind of sad, isn't it? All the wisdom in the world, and yet this wisdom had little to no power to affect his choices. Solomon in his wisdom knew things that Solomon in his experience couldn't live out. And so the man who had wisdom directly from God ends life on a sour note. He turns aside from worshipping God alone in order to worship at the altars of false gods with his many wives (1 Kings 11:4-6). His own son Rehoboam is a weak and wicked ruler, having adopted none of the wisdom his father displayed. Within a handful of years, the kingdom that David created and passed off to Solomon has become divided, with each half-kingdom doing what was evil in the Lord's sight. This was Solomon's legacy.

Solomon's beliefs and his behaviors were miles apart. Sound familiar at all? If nothing else, Solomon should be a case study for all of us that our problem, our addiction, is not in knowledge. We don't need to learn more about our problem. We don't need more words and insight from books. (I know, an ironic thing for me to say as I write a book!) We can't learn our way into recovery. Simply put, wisdom and knowledge are not enough to overcome the gap that has developed in our divided personality.

So how do we change? How do we overcome the gap between what we know and what we do? That, my friend, is the ultimate subject of this book and we will keep unpacking that theme one chapter at a time.

OUR STORY: MAYBE WE DID LEARN IT ALL IN KINDERGARTEN...

Before we go on to how real change occurs, I want to make sure we fully investigate this step on the Addictive Journey. Much like we overlook the circumstances in our lives present at birth, so also we can easily overlook our childhood experiences and our early understanding of sexuality. I am convinced that our most influential views of sexuality come from our childhood years. In fact, I see men all the time living out a version of sexuality they learned as little boys and have just never changed. Sadly, we would never expect to have the same methods of tying our shoes, spelling words, or the weekly bath routine that we had as seven-year-olds, but many men are operating on essentially the same sexual message they learned at that time.

Let me illustrate it this way. Every family has a style or a way of approaching sex. Imagine it if you will as an "X" and "Y" axis, where the X axis is a continuum between moral and immoral and the Y axis is a continuum between open and closed. Every family falls somewhere along these lines. They are either moral, with a highly developed sense of right and wrong when it comes to human sexuality, or immoral, with no set boundaries on sexuality other than perhaps what is legal, and maybe not even then. They are also either open, talking easily and freely about sex, or they are closed, with sex being the taboo topic that everyone tiptoes around. This creates four family dynamics, each one unique. See where you think your family of origin would fit. If your family background was pretty scattered, use your primary home environment between the ages of five and twelve as a reference point.

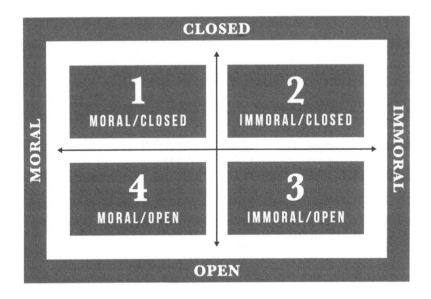

1) MORAL AND CLOSED

This would be the most common description of the "good Christian family." If you grew up in a home where both parents went to church, this is probably your family. In this quadrant, we assume others in the family know what's right and do what's right in the area of sexuality. We believe the same things and hear the same things preached, so there's no reason to discuss views at home. In general, this family doesn't talk about sex at all, except to emphasize what's right, and more importantly, what's wrong.

This kind of environment lends itself to a couple of extremes. In his book, *Real Marriage*, Mark Driscoll gives a helpful distinction on the different ways we view sex.[4] He says that we can see sex as gross, as god, or as gift. In a moral and closed environment, we will tend toward the first two extremes, either seeing sex as gross or as god. In a home with high moral standards, sex is most frequently discussed in negative terms—pointing out the sinful behavior of others, condemning the sexuality of culture, or teaching the "thou shalt nots" of Scripture. When this restrictive side of sex is the bulk of a person's at-home training, they can begin to view sex as something dangerous, dirty, and unpleasant.

The other extreme is for sex to become a god. In the moral and closed environment, a person receives contradictory messages. Sex is everywhere around them in culture, but it is never discussed at home. This hush-hush approach makes them gravitate toward the holy grail of sexuality as something mystical, secretive, and risky. Rather than teaching a healthy view of sexuality, this environment inadvertently creates a heightened misunderstanding of sex as powerful, taboo, and rebellious. Thus, unsurprisingly, the adventure-seeking brain of young males will run after sex!

2) IMMORAL AND CLOSED
In the second quadrant, the family assumes everyone's screwed up when it comes to sex. Mom, or Dad, has likely been married a few times and had numerous other short-term relationships. Sexual relations among adults is just a given, and the primary teacher in this environment is culture, followed closely by learned behavior. The parent(s) have little health or wholeness when it comes to their sexuality, so they feel they have nothing to teach. They believe their kids will learn the way they did through experience—but they certainly don't want to talk about their experiences. *And what good will come of talking about sex when we're so messed up. We can't teach or help because we're so hurt*, they think.

3) IMMORAL AND OPEN
In this third quadrant, sex is common and casual. Dad's stash of Playboy and other adult magazines isn't a secret, or may even be

left lying around; sexually explicit videos are left out or turned on even when children may be present; parental figures or adults in the home joke frequently about sex and talk or brag openly about their behaviors and their bodies. This environment is "open" in that sex is a regular and normal part of everyday communication, but because this environment is also immoral, with few if any rules governing sexual behavior, the open communication is not healthy. Once again, for children in this home, sex can become a god—as a human experience to be sought out as regularly as possible—or sex can become gross, a backlash against the perversions and crassness on display.

4) MORAL AND OPEN

This is the one quadrant where sex becomes a gift. People from moral and open homes are able to talk about sex, both the negative aspects *and* the healthy, positive side. Kids are given freedom to ask questions, process their experiences, and relate their struggles. Dads and moms are able to be honest about joys and pains, victories and failures, all without being unnecessarily descriptive or revealing. Honesty is valued and weakness or sin is dealt with in grace and truth. This kind of environment, in my opinion, is rare. If you grew up in this kind of a home, where sex was neither avoided as taboo nor flung around as common, then you were blessed with a much healthier view of human sexuality than most.

In this quadrant, sex is understood as a gift when received as God intended it. We understand that God created our human bodies and He gave us sex, not only for the procreation of our race, but also for our mutual pleasure and enjoyment in the marriage relationship. God uniquely designed the male and female bodies to bond physically, mentally and emotionally with one another for a lifetime. This understanding of sex as a gift helps children form a healthy view of themselves and an ability to recognize the ways in which our world has warped this gift into something trivial and cheap. A moral and open environment creates a longing to keep oneself pure for marriage in order to enjoy the fullest expression of this gift.

This is a brief summary and overview of these four quadrants. Certainly more could be said and far more detail added, but I think this gives you enough information to quickly assess and determine where your family of origin lands. From this perspective, can you begin to see the tremendous impact your childhood environment had on shaping the way you view sex? From our childhood experiences, we get messages about ourselves and about sex that may have little to do with God's truth, but at young ages we can't process the vast disconnect between the two. Unless we grow up in the fourth quadrant, a healthy open and moral environment, we grow up twisted in our view of sex. Unable to process what we are experiencing, our brain helps us out by creating another personality—the sexual personality— that stays hidden from public view. The freedom that Jesus promised is all about reconnecting these two sides; it's all about becoming whole and holy even in the area of our sexuality.

TO TALK OR NOT TO TALK

For many of us, the idea of talking to our kids about sex and human sexuality can be very intimidating. Where do we begin? What do we say? How do we not make our kids feel awkward and embarrassed? I think one of our struggles in talking to our kids is actually a root fear we have about being adequate to the task. Do we have a right to talk about healthy sexuality with our kids when we feel pretty messed up ourselves, or when our past has left a wake of wreckage?

A unique story in the life of King David (Solomon's dad) that rarely gets discussed has a rather graphic beginning that can be challenging to preach in a church setting. One of David's sons (Amnon) rapes his half sister (Tamar). When David hears about this, he becomes "very angry" (2 Samuel 13:21). But that's it! No mention of intervention or action taken against Amnon. No follow-up to protect Tamar or see retribution paid. In this historic Jewish society, Amnon has essentially destroyed all future prospects of marriage for Tamar, and thus ended her hopes of any significant social standing. As if the rape itself wasn't enough, the ongoing stigma for Tamar would have been devastating. And the Bible says that David only got "very angry." He takes no action.

Why? This story is placed in Scripture one chapter after David is confronted over his own sin with Bathsheba. The proximity of stories to one another in Scripture has more to do with significance and less to do with timeline. I think it's fair to say that David fails to challenge and correct Amnon because he feels he has no right. After all, he's just recently impregnated a married woman and had her husband murdered to try and cover it up. How can he possibly talk to his son about this rape?

But here's the deal: David's failure to confront and correct his own son will cause him far more pain and suffering than his own personal sin ever did. As a result of this story, Absalom (Tamar's brother, Amnon's half-brother and David's full son) will kill Amnon. He will rebel against his father David and take the kingdom and Jerusalem for himself. He will sleep with David's concubines in public view and end up in a vicious battle with his father's men. In the end, thousands of Israel's fathers and sons will die in the feud between father and son. All of it, I believe could have been avoided had David taken action himself to discipline Amnon. Far greater devastation occurred in his life because he stood aloof and simply "got angry."

While I doubt a scenario of this magnitude will ever play out in your life, we can learn from this. Our unwillingness to confront our own children with grace and truth can lead to far greater pain and suffering in our lives than our own personal sin ever did. I realize you may have made some poor choices in your past and feel you have little to "teach" your son or daughter. But you are *the parent*. God has placed you in that role to train your kids in the way they should go, and this includes the area of human sexuality.

You may not be able to say, "Do as I did," but you can be honest about the pain you have experienced and what you learned from it. You can open Scripture and show them the beauty of God's plan. You don't need to be an expert; that's not your role. But you *are* the parent, and talking to your kids in normal, healthy ways about sex must be part of that role. So fathers, talk to your boys about sex! And not just the one-time birds and the bees talk, either. I mean help them process what they are seeing and experiencing in the world around them. Mothers, talk to your daughters about sex. And dads to daughters and moms to sons. Teach God's plan, because you are the parent! This is the role God has given you. Will it be easy? Not necessarily. But God will meet you and help you as you take this to Him.

THE LINCHPIN: THE TWO BECOME ONE

It is in childhood that the disconnect between what we did and what we believed first got its start. We did what we knew we weren't supposed to do or didn't want to do. And when our brains were uncertain about how to process that data, we shaped two identities to accommodate—one for others to see and one to house the sexual memories, experiences, and pain. But here is the awesome truth: God has never seen you as two, only as one. God knows and loves the real you. No matter what your childhood has taught you about sex and how you may have isolated yourself from some memories or behaviors, God has been there all along, and He is at work to make you whole again.

We can trust Him because in His all-seeing knowledge of us, He has never turned away or run from us. Our past may have told us, "Don't talk. Don't tell." But we need to talk and we need to tell in order for God to meet us there. We need to discover the gift of sex that God has given us so we can see all of the ways in which our past and our culture have twisted it into something He never intended. This is His holy work of making all things, including you, new again. We are now His holy work, and He will see it through until the end.

Whatever is good and perfect is a gift coming down to us from God our Father, who created all the lights in the heavens. He never changes or casts a shifting shadow. He chose to give birth to us by giving us his true word. And we, out of all creation, became his prized possession.
James 1:17-18

CHAPTER THREE | ADOLESCENCE

If our most powerful views about human sexuality are formed in childhood, then our most significant patterns of sexuality are formed in adolescence. During the teen years, we begin to train our brains how to react to sexual stimuli. Even more important than the fact that we learn *how* to react is for us to see *why* we head that way. Why does the pattern of our life move us toward sexually driven behaviors, particularly when some of these behaviors violate our sense of morality or faith in God?

The teen years are fertile ground for coping behaviors of all kinds. While "coping" may sound like a clinical, psychobabble kind of word, it's really not. A coping behavior, simply put, is any activity we engage in to either avoid pain or create pleasure. We cope all the time, in some ways that are positive and healthy and in other ways that are not.

Not only are our teen years filled with some of the most radical physical changes occurring in us, these are also years when more is required of us than ever before. During these years, we are expected to excel in our education; find hobbies, clubs, or teams to develop our skills; learn the ropes of boy/girl relationships; and start answering the penultimate question of what we plan to do with the rest of our life. The stakes of failure or success feel very high. For most of us, the outcome is some of both. We learn where we can succeed and achieve, but in the process of discovering these places we also encounter failure, rejection, and loss. Either experience—success or failure—can be the trigger point for coping patterns.

Just before my teen years began, my family moved from Greybull, Wyoming (remember the great place to be from?), to Helena, Montana. While these two western locations may not trigger much of a reaction for some readers, this was big change for my family and me. In Greybull, the entire middle school had been arranged in six different classrooms along one single hallway. My graduating class, had my family tarried in this town, would have been about thirty-five. I felt like a big fish in a small pond. I was already learning to perform my way into acceptance—academically, musically, and athletically. For the most part, I was succeeding. I had visions of grandeur about how I would one day grow up to be a three-sport superstar: all-state caliber in football, basketball, and track. In the sixth grade, the high school coaches were already watching me and talking to me about the roles I would one day fill. Performing felt good! It filled a void and started to create within me a powerful sense of identity. I *was* my performance.

After living in Greybull for sixteen years as pastor of the church, Dad and Mom felt called to take a struggling congregation in Helena. Not too unlike their beginnings in Greybull, a small crowd of about twenty saints was managing to keep the doors open while they looked for a new pastor.

Moving to Helena meant my middle school was automatically ten times larger. Coming from my small, single-hall experience, C.R. Anderson Middle School looked cavernous. The graduating class size here was estimated to be around 350. No longer was I the big fish in a little pond; overnight I had become the little fish in a big pond. And what's more, I was new to these waters.

This move occurred when I was twelve years old. I was already trying to figure out who I was and what I was good at.

Now the question that loomed larger than ever was, "How will I make a name for myself?" I knew one answer and one answer only: Perform. The pressure of making a name for myself pushed me to excel even more. By my sophomore year in high school, I was playing three sports, singing in the top-level choir, playing saxophone in the top-level band, and carrying a 4.0 grade average. It was through these activities that I defined myself. I found how good it felt to be noticed, loved, admired, and cheered.

What I also discovered was that no amount of success could satisfy my search for an identity. Perhaps you happened upon this realization as well. Whether your approach was performance, or popularity, or running with cool kids, the skater kids or hacky sack group; whether you tried to fit in by your looks, your grades, or your goofing off, you found, as I did, that this was never quite enough. In spite of the tremendous success I was having, something inside of me hungered for more. Achieving my goals didn't suffice.

Alongside the victories, I also knew the pain of failure, rejection, and loss. I dropped game-winning touchdown passes. I got benched and yelled at by coaches. No matter how smart I thought I was, there were always others that were better, brighter, and more praised. If the success wasn't enough to define me, the failures certainly opened the inner chasm even wider.

It was at this time, I discovered how the excitement of lust and passion brought comfort. Like most teenage boys, the onset of hormones at puberty made me feel very attracted to women. But also like most teenage boys, I felt completely insecure in how to actually have a relationship with one. So it was easier to be drawn to images. For a while, images in a Target ad or a commercial would suffice, but these images only fed a desire inside; something inside felt so good and so alive when my brain was turned on like this. The images lured me in with false promises that a sense of identity and worth would come if I only had a little more.

Pornography became very real to me during the summer of 1993. That year, our family took a vacation through the badlands of South Dakota. The trip included stops at Mount Rushmore, Deadwood, and the famed Passion Play in Spearfish. My older sister was headed to college that fall, so it was our last hurrah before life began to separate us.

One of our stops was at an outdoor flea market or bazaar somewhere between the stone heads of Mount Rushmore and the free ice water at Wall Drug. Our family was always on the lookout for good deals on cheap stuff, so the van pulled over almost without prompting. As we all spilled out of the car that day, my mind was already searching—searching for something to make me feel good. The one place I never felt particularly good about myself was with my family. They knew me too well to be impressed by my performance. So the one good thing I had going for me everywhere else—performance—seemed to fail me at home. I put on my best show for those who knew me best because I feared allowing them to see my dark side.

As the family perused the tables of cheap commodities, I found myself separated from them. I wandered aimlessly through the rows of vendors looking for something to catch my eye. What finally did was a stack of magazines, and on the top of the pile was the image of a woman scantily clothed. Her eyes had a look that said, "It just gets better inside." My heart began to race as I contemplated my options. Up to this point in my life, I knew that such a thing as pornography existed, but I had never held the material personally. Because of this, I was too scared and naive to even consider purchasing it. That would be to admit to another human being—the seller—that I actually wanted to look. To admit that I wanted to look was an admission of evil in my mind. So, as strange and contradictory as it may seem, I decided to steal the magazine. Brazen theft in broad daylight!

How on earth I convinced myself that purchasing a copy was wrong, but swiping the magazine was okay is beyond me. The rationale of teenage boys doesn't necessarily make sense. I was driven to find something stimulating but not brave enough to own up to that desire. So instead of asking, I shoved the top magazine under my shirt and walked away while no one was looking. Little did I know that in this moment, I was opening my heart to an enslavement that would last for seventeen years.

Looking at that magazine later when I was alone, I experienced what I would describe as a veritable crush of emotions in an instant. On the one hand, I was overwhelmed with the excitement and energy that God intended for us to feel when seeing a naked body for the first time. (Of course, this was out of order from God's timeline; nonetheless, my brain responded as God designed it to.) On the other hand, a wave of guilt, shame, and nausea came over me that I had never experienced before. How could I do this? I was a good kid! I wanted to do what was right! And I even liked it! Shouldn't I be repulsed by "sin?" In one moment, I experienced as high a pleasure and as low a condemnation as I had ever experienced before. The pleasure feeling made me want to find more. The condemnation made me promise I never would. This set me up in an addictive cycle for years to come.

Now let me pause a moment and trace the path I took to this point. I now realize this was not an isolated moment of giving in to temptation. The path I took is significant because it likely parallels a similar path in your life, even if the scenarios and stories are completely different. I was born in circumstances that set me up with a strong desire to be noticed. I found that being the good, successful kid got me noticed. But I had also learned that sexuality felt gross and such experiences could never be shared. I was set up to perform; I learned to perform; and I found that performance wasn't enough. I also learned that sex was powerful; guilt should be hidden; and exposing weakness would undermine my performance-driven exterior. In the summer of 1993, all of these threads came together when I discovered the powerful world of pornography.

Following this first experience, I began to learn that when I felt restless, purposeless, or alone, lust and pornography—and all of the emotions associated with it—would fill the gap. No matter how much I achieved or accomplished, it was never enough to answer the deeper questions of my heart. I found myself developing patterns of sin. Late at night after football and basketball road trips, when my performance had failed again to define me, stopping at a local convenience store to buy a magazine became a convenient substitute for feeling good. On lazy Sunday afternoons or moments where I wanted to procrastinate on real work, escaping into a vivid fantasy life brought a sense of accomplishment and relief. The false reality of feeling attractive to the images of beautiful women on a page or in my mind brought the satisfaction I longed for most, if only for a moment.

But this relief was always temporary and was followed by the walloping punch of my morality and spirituality. I felt guilt and shame beyond belief. How could I be so weak and sinful? How could I long so strongly for something I knew to be wrong? I believed in my heart I was twisted. I began to see myself internally, in my heart and in my mind, as a bad person. And so the need to perform only grew because I had to hide what I was feeling inside. As discussed in Chapter 2, I had a split identity because the dark side could hold the secrets in, but it also kept real love out. All of the love, admiration, and praise rang hollow in my ears because I knew the "me" that others did not.

Before you start assuming that I was remarkably introspective and aware for a teenager, I would like to point out that I was actually unaware of any of this at the time. In my mind, I was doing what teenagers do. In fact, I was doing far less than most of my teammates were bragging about in the locker room. I was blind to the deeper needs in my heart that were driving my behavior.

But if we want to set our hearts and minds straight, we must be willing to go back to those years and experiences and ask ourselves and others what was really happening. As C. S. Lewis puts it in his work, *The Great Divorce*, "I do not think that all who choose wrong roads perish; but their rescue consists in being put back on the right road. A sum can be put right: but only *by going back till you find the error* and working it afresh from that point, never by simply going on. Evil can be undone, but it cannot 'develop' into good. Time does not heal it. The spell must be unwound, bit by bit"[5] (italics mine).

If we want to be set free from sexual addiction and temptation, we need more than fresh behavioral techniques or Internet filtering software. These things have great value, but real change is the result of becoming a whole person again. Sin causes a divide between the public self and the hidden self; grace is all about going back and discovering where the divide occurred, so that the love of Jesus can heal that chasm.

GOD'S STORY: A NEW WAY OF SEEING

One of the things God is at work to do in us is restore the divide between what we see on the inside and what everyone else sees on the outside. We create this divide to protect ourselves. We create the divide so that we can do things privately or in some sectors of our life that we would never do in others. In this process, we begin to see one side or the other as the "real" us. We gravitate toward that side becoming the whole us, but we don't know how to do it. This is where God comes along. He reveals that our deepest need is not to choose between one side and the other, but to see the two sides become one.

One story in Scripture that grabs my heart is that of Mephibosheth. This character was never taught in my Sunday school years. Perhaps the teachers found his name too difficult for tooth-losing first graders to pronounce, or maybe he just got lost in the shuffle between his more heroic and prominent relatives, Saul and Jonathan. Though his story may be unfamiliar to you, it has powerful implications for us all. This is his story from 2 Samuel:

David finally became king. Years earlier, God had promised David he would sit on the throne of Israel. What God had not revealed to David was that he would endure years of harassment and punishment at the hand of King Saul, his predecessor. In a tragic fight with the Philistines, King Saul and three of his sons were killed in the heat of battle, including his oldest son and heir to the throne, Jonathan. This paved the way for David to finally ascend to God's promised position. In quick succession, David secured an army, conquered Jerusalem and established it as his capital, defeated the Philistines, and brought the Ark of the Covenant into the city. His position as king was firmly established and a dynasty was in the making.

At this time in his reign, David had an interesting request. He summoned Ziba, a former slave of King Saul, into the throne room and asked, "Are any of King Saul's family members still alive?" And who would know better than a high-ranking slave of Saul's house? It was common practice in those days for a new king to annihilate the family of the former king so as to eliminate any and all competing claims to the throne. So for Ziba, this question certainly had an ominous feel. He replied cautiously, knowing that to hide the information would likely mean his own death, "Yes, one of Jonathan's sons is still alive, but he is crippled."

There he is—that's Mephibosheth. His introduction to the king doesn't even include his name, only his infirmity. He is crippled. A brief mention of how Mephibosheth became crippled appears in 2 Samuel 4. On the day that Saul and Jonathan were killed, his nurse scooped him up to flee the city, fearing that he would be killed to protect the throne of the future king. But on her way out of town, she dropped him. It must have been quite a fall, because now, many years later, Mephibosheth is still crippled. And his deformity has become his identity. Ziba didn't even tell the king his name, just what's wrong with him.

David seemed to pay no attention to that. The news of a surviving relative excited King David who asked, "Where is he?" (2 Samuel 9:4). "In Lo-debar," replied Ziba, certain that he has signed the death warrant for Saul and Jonathan's final heir. David sent for him at once.

Try and imagine this story from Mephibosheth's point view. Since he was five years old, he had been living in Lo-debar, an out-of-the-way place if there ever was one. The name can mean "no pasture," or even better "no word" and "no communication." Mephibosheth had been living in this out-of-the-way desolate place. Once the son of the future king, he was now a wanted fugitive. He had done his best to stay hidden in an off-the-beaten-path hole, so he could go on with his life. But he was crippled in both feet, a constant reminder of his past and the death that awaited him if he were ever discovered. His beliefs about this had forced him to separate from the life and the people he used to know. He believed that isolation and fear were better than what awaited him in Jerusalem.

One day, soldiers showed up from Jerusalem bearing the insignia of King David. At long last, the day Mephibosheth had feared since he was five years old had come to pass. He had been discovered. In some ways, it was actually a relief to quit hiding, even though he believed his life was over. He was taken directly to Jerusalem and told to prepare himself to meet the King face to face.

Mephibosheth was brought before David. He bowed low and said, "I am your servant" (2 Samuel 9:6). He came in fear, sure that David had brought him to kill him. David was now the most powerful man in the world and no challenger to his throne could be left alive. Mephibosheth knelt and prepared for the blow to his neck that would bring his life to a quick end.

But what Mephibosheth didn't know was that David had made an oath. He swore a promise to his best friend Jonathan that he would bless his family as his own. So while Mephibosheth feared death, the king was planning to bless. The words that come out of King David's mouth were not "off with his head!" but instead, "welcome home." David gave back to Mephibosheth all of the land that Saul once held. This would certainly have been a large holding. And how does a man with two crippled feet care for all that land? David calls for Ziba the servant and says to him, "You served King Saul and now you and your whole house will serve this man." That must have been quite a shock for Mephibosheth, since Ziba had fifteen sons and twenty servants!

But that's not all. David could have stopped here. He had been more than generous already with Mephibosheth by taking him from nowhere and giving him great wealth. But David's desire to bless went well beyond material, financial blessing. At the heart of this blessing was a relationship, built on the friendship that David had with Jonathan. He said to Mephibosheth, "You will live here at the palace with me and eat at my table." David embraced him as family—as one of his own sons.

Can you imagine this transformation? One morning, Mephibosheth woke up in a forgotten, "no-word" place, afraid of being found out and discovered. By the end of the day, he's eating at the table with the king and being treated as one of David's own sons. Mephibosheth thought he was a dead dog worthy of execution, but the king saw him as a valued child. The king saw what he could not see. How did this all happen? There are three aspects of Mephibosheth's story that I want to highlight as they relate to our own stories:

1) Mephibosheth felt defined by his wound, but the king defined him by a promise. Mephibosheth called himself a "dead dog" in this story. I love that! How often have I felt like a dead dog in my places of weakness, brokenness, and sin? What this reveals to me about Mephibosheth, though, is that his woundedness had become his identity. He used to be the son of a king, but now he was just a wounded, dead dog worthy of nothing. But that's not what the king saw at all! David can only see him *through* the promise he made to Jonathan. David didn't see the weakness or the infirmity; he was only concerned with the promise he had made to Jonathan to treat his children like his own.

2) Though Mephibosheth feared exposure, this exposure actually brought life. Mephibosheth had spent his life hiding from his past and hiding from his true identity. He believed that if he were discovered it would mean death for him. But the moment he was discovered and truly known was the moment where his life began. He hobbled out of the shadows of Lo-debar and began to feast with the king. He believed the king longed to destroy him, when in truth the king wanted to give him abundant life.

3) At the center of the heart of King David's blessing is the desire for relationship. David blessed Mephibosheth, not because he was worthy of blessing, but because of whose son he was. Mephibosheth's lineage as a child of Jonathan meant far more to David than the customary practices of eliminating the competition. He invited Mephibosheth to his table and blessed him.

Every day Mephibosheth sat and dined with the king. His woundedness didn't disappear. In fact, at the very end of the story, the Bible reminds us one more time that he was crippled in both feet. But this deformity no longer defined Mephibosheth. It was his seat at the table of the king that mattered most.

OUR STORY: INTRODUCING YOURSELF TO JESUS

Can you see yourself in Mephibosheth's story? His story is written all over our lives. Somewhere in our lives, we have been dropped. We have been hurt, wounded, and deformed by the actions and behaviors of ourselves or others. This may not have even been intentional or malicious. Sometimes it is, and those wounds can be the most obvious and also the most painful. But in many other ways, we have simply been dropped and damaged along the way by other humans who are just like us.

A busy parent doesn't intend to neglect us, but we feel lost in the shuffle. A performance-oriented dad isn't consciously thinking about having a high standard for us, but we constantly feel the need to jump higher for his approval. The divorce wasn't our fault or our choosing, but it has deeply affected our identity. An older sibling doesn't see how his lifestyle and attitude left us feeling inferior and weak. Others were busy doing what they thought was best, and along the way we got injured. We were dropped. We became crippled.

And in that place of injury, lust and pornography present themselves as a way to feel good about life. For at least a brief moment, we find respite from ourselves through the artificial high of sex. We forget about our Lo-debar; we forget about being crippled and fearful and give in to something that makes it all go away for a brief time. But in the end, we are left feeling further away from others than ever before. So we make ourselves comfortable in Lo-debar, defined by our weaknesses and fearful of being discovered.

But God in His grace has come looking for us! We may not have been looking for Him; in fact, we may have been doing our best to hide from Him! Still, the good and loving King doesn't see us through our deformity, but through His promise. He's aware of the wounds and knows that only through restored relationship with Him will we be made right again.

One of the problems with living in Lo-debar so long is that we have firmly entrenched ourselves in split identities. We construct them so well over time, and rely on them so strongly, that we actually believe the real "us" is the one everyone sees. The dark side, the hidden and isolated side, we see as a deviation of what we really are, and we wish that side of us would just go away.

But what if the hidden side feels more truly us than anything else? What if the dark side of you is more honestly you than the projected image? "Ugh," we might say, "that's not encouraging. That part of me is pretty sick and twisted by life. If that's really me then I'm in big trouble."

A while back, I was struggling with this idea of the two sides of me: the one that everyone loved because that side was smart, funny, responsible, and caring, and the one that very few knew, but I despised because that side was selfish, lustful, deceptive, and rude. I had read in a book somewhere that one of the best ways to "deal" with our dark side was to expose it to the light, to introduce the worst of ourselves to Jesus, so that He could shine the light of His glory and grace on us. I supposed that in the light, the weak and selfish part of me would shrivel up and disappear. Jesus would finally make him go away.

I can recall that I was on a run while thinking this through. I do some of my best thinking on my feet. Something about being away from other distractions and out on my own helps me focus on God more than at any other time. On this occasion, I was praying through this idea, thinking it couldn't hurt to at least try it out, to attempt to expose my darkness to His light. So I said, "Jesus, this is the me that I hate. This is the me that leads me into sin and pornography, into lust and lies. Here he is. Can you make him go away now?"

But what happened next surprised me. I can only recall a handful of times when I am certain that Jesus spoke to me in real time. Usually, I have to look back a long time later to recognize His voice. But in that moment, Jesus said, "That's the Nick I died for. I didn't die for the best of you, but for the very worst of you. That's the you that I love and long to restore." The emotion I felt in that moment was overwhelming. It slowed me to a walk and nearly took me to my knees. I was too proud to be seen publicly kneeling in front of city hall where I happened to be at that moment, but on the inside I was facedown before God. When I exposed the worst of who I was to Jesus, I was astounded to find that this was the me He loved enough to die for.

The emotion was so powerful because I had honestly never

considered that Jesus loved this me and perhaps this was more truly me than I had ever known. In the place of my woundedness, my Lo-debar, I found a deep truth: This was the real me that had been dropped as a kid and had spent a lifetime hiding and performing for fear of more pain and rejection. When this crippled soul was exposed to the penetrating light of Christ's love, it filled me with hope and joy. If Jesus could love this side of me enough to die, then there was hope that this very same side could be healed and changed.

Think about this for a moment: The hidden you is more real than anything you have ever projected for others to see and to love. In projecting this public you, which is really a false self, you insulate your hidden self from exposure, disgrace, and humiliation. But in this attempt to isolate, you also insulate yourself from experiencing true love and life-shifting grace. Like Mephibosheth, we need to be brought into the presence of a King who cares for us more than we can imagine. Though we may have spent our whole lives fearing His wrath and punishment, it is only when we are fully present to Him that we begin to understand His all-consuming love for us. His love is not based on our performance or on the goodness of our projected self, but on the eternal truth of His promises. He cares more about whose son we are than about anything we have ever done.

For all of this to happen, though, we have to step out of isolation. We have to allow ourselves to be brought out of hiding and into the light. That can be a very scary prospect, especially when we've spent a lifetime hiding in places like Lo-debar. So how do we come and take a seat at the King's table? How do we leave our places of hiding and walk into His light? This is the piece of the addictive story we'll turn to in the next chapter.

And I have to warn you, I spent a long time getting this next part wrong before I ever got it right.

THE LINCHPIN: KNOWING WHO YOU ARE

When Jesus promised His listeners freedom (John 8), not everyone got it. In fact, by the end of the message, a portion of the crowd had picked up stones to end His life on the spot. I've preached some poor sermons before that may have bored people into a slumber, but stirring people to stone you takes real talent. What could Jesus have possibly said to cause such a commotion? He was promising freedom, wasn't He?

But here's the issue: Those who picked up stones couldn't accept the fact that they were slaves. They held onto an ideal that their physical birth into the Jewish line made them sons of Abraham, and according to God's Word, sons of Abraham could not be slaves. So, when Jesus promised to set them free, they couldn't even see their slavery.

We learn from this that a case of mistaken identity will always keep us from experiencing the best of what Jesus has for us. Our case of mistaken identity occurs when we believe that the false self we construct and show around to others is the true us. This "good side" has little need to be free. We just need that other side to go away!

Until God's love penetrates all the way to the core of our hidden self, His love will only be a concept or an idea that we nod to in church. His love won't really change us if we believe He only loves the projected self. Who wouldn't love that side of us? But it is when we introduce the hidden self to Jesus and find that He runs to us, we begin to change. We can become whole with one identity: in Christ. This is the King's promise to us. The honest truth is that we are not the worst of us or the best of us; we are somewhere in between and somehow parts of both and somehow really neither at all. In Christ, the two become one. The separated self becomes the whole self. And when these two sides become whole, Jesus starts to make a lot more sense. Then you will know the truth, and the truth will set you free!

> *But when the right time came, God sent his Son, born of a woman, subject to the law. God sent him to buy freedom for us who were slaves to the law, so that he could adopt us as his very own children. And because we are his children, God has sent the Spirit of his Son into our hearts, prompting us to call out, "Abba, Father." Now you are no longer a slave but God's own child. And since you are his child, God has made you his heir.*
> Galatians 4:4-7

CHAPTER FOUR | MERE ACCOUNTABILITY

Confession is nothing. And confession is everything. I feel like a tightrope walker as I write this chapter. Somehow, I hope to delicately balance these two ideas that seem contradictory. How could both be true at the same time? Though we may not be accustomed to living with such diametrically opposed ideas working in harmony, I hope by the end of this chapter you'll see that it's true. I know from my own story that it is.

One common aspect of this journey is our desire to hide what we have done from others. But this hiding creates a tension, a division of soul that I have mentioned frequently. We can go a couple of directions with this tension. Some find a way to insulate their soul, or their mind, from the feelings of shame and guilt and "succeed" in living a double life, where their conscious day-to-day relationships are held separate from the underside of their behaviors. The other direction is to live constantly with this awareness that we are not who we say we are, and this feeling creates a growing burden in our souls to come clean.

This was always my bent. Try as I may, I could never keep the feelings of guilt at bay and ignore them for long. Sooner or later, the remorse of things done would bubble to the surface and I would spill my "secrets." I would have made a good Catholic; confession became a regular part of my life.

The first time I found the courage to fess up to my sin of lust was after youth group one night as a young teen. After most everyone had left the room, I asked the youth leaders if they could stay and talk. I remember feeling as though my heart were going to beat right out of my chest as they closed the door and asked, "What's up?" I felt like their whole perception of me was about to be shattered, and I was very fearful of what they would ask me to do next—who else they would require me to tell. All I knew, though, was that I had to tell someone because the weight of this secret was wrecking me inside.

In a tearful confession, I poured out my heart about lust and masturbation. At this time, I hadn't even discovered the pornography side of things. Even in this confession, though, I am certain I cleaned things up and told my story in a way that didn't make me look too bad or twisted. It's sad, really, how our desire to look good to others colors our best attempts to get real with them. Though I was confessing openly, I was still half-hidden. Regardless of how much or how little truth I got out there, this was a huge step of opening up to the reality of my actions.

Their reaction was nothing short of superb. They didn't get a shocked look on their faces and call me a freak. They didn't laugh or point fingers. They didn't march me right up to my dad's office and demand I tell him. They listened. They nodded. They thanked me for sharing. (Something I found so bizarre at the time.) They encouraged me with words from Scripture and stories from their own lives. They prayed with me and for me. They became my first real experience of grace on display and they modeled it well.

And then we all went home.

I thought to myself, *Finally. It's out there. Now I will be free!* I took to heart Jesus' words that I had acknowledged truth and I believed that truth would set me free. But the opposite actually proved to be true. No one followed up with me. No one gave me a real plan for how to deal with these thoughts. I don't blame them because at the same time, I made zero change in my own life. I believed that confession itself would set me free. And if I wasn't free, I expected my confessors would come and rescue me. Oh how I wanted to be rescued!

Without sufficient resources to truly change in a deep way, the behavior continued; in fact, not only did it continue, it grew worse and deeper, now with more shame and guilt than ever before. Now other people knew about it and were praying for me, but I still couldn't stop.

Prior to this, I had been hiding the behavior from people who didn't know it existed. Now it was a whole new experience to keep the behavior from people who did know it was a problem. It felt doubly deceptive to withhold new missteps from them. So began a painful cycle of acting out, hiding behavior, and living in shame until I could bear it no more and another confession would occur.

Oh, did it occur: To a counselor at a youth conference as part of an altar call, who prayed, affirmed, and encouraged. To a college friend that became an accountability group of four—who all prayed, affirmed, and encouraged. To my fiancée—who prayed, affirmed, and encouraged. To the college student life dean—who prayed, affirmed, and encouraged. To my senior pastor, my ordination mentor, my elders (twice!), and to the men in my small group—who all prayed, affirmed, and encouraged.

Through it all, I remained unchanged. Stuck. Oh sure, I learned some valuable lessons about grace and love. I saw in them how to offer forgiveness and encouragement. I would be straightened out by all these confessional experiences like a reset button and walk in a time of purity. But sooner or later, I would return to the behavior like the proverbial dog going back to its vomit (Proverbs 26:11)! No one rescued me and nothing changed. This actually deepened the guilt and shame. All these people knew, were praying, and wanted to help, and yet I couldn't quit. *What is wrong with me?* I thought. Performance was my MO (method of operation) in life, and I was failing miserably to perform well in this area.

GOD'S STORY: TRUE CONFESSION

The last thing I would want you to think is that I am against confession. Even though my story is a long litany of confessions that didn't result in change, I fully believe that confession was—and is—the right thing to do and is a significant step in changing a behavior. Confession is a direct assault on our desire to look good and maintain a projected false self. Confession breaks the barriers we place between us and God, and between ourselves and others.

Without a doubt, Scripture commends and commands us to enter into confession with others. Probably the most classic passage on confession is in James 5:16: "Confess your sins to each other and pray for each other so that you may be healed." There it is in black and white: Confession leads to healing! God's Word teaches that confession is absolutely crucial to faith and forgiveness. "But if we confess our sins to him [God], he is faithful and just to forgive us our sins and to cleanse us from all wickedness" (1 John 1:9). And then there's Psalm 32, a great penitent hymn: "When I refused to confess my sin, my body wasted away, and I groaned all day long. Day and night your hand of discipline was heavy on me. My strength evaporated like water in the summer heat" (vv. 3-4).

Have you felt the life-draining weight of unconfessed sin? I know I have! But there's hope: "Finally, I confessed all my sins to you and stopped trying to hide my guilt. I said to myself, 'I will confess my rebellion to the Lord.' And you forgave me! All my guilt is gone" (Psalm 32:5). When Israel confessed their sins to God during the time of the judges, He routinely responded by sending a deliverer. When Israel confessed their sins to Samuel (1 Samuel 7:6), God delivered them miraculously from the Philistines. When people confessed their sins to John the Baptist, he ushered them into the new Kingdom of God through baptism. When we confess our sins to Jesus, He forgives, heals, and sets us right with God. Confession can do some pretty amazing things!

But what I see in Scripture is that the concept of confession is only half of the equation. Take a brief walk through some biblical examples with me.

People in the Bible understood that sin cost something. The entire Jewish sacrificial system was a complex metaphor for the extreme cost of sin. The concept of confession was far more than an admission of guilt; it included a payment or restitution.

Consider Leviticus 5. (You know, that book of the Bible after Exodus that always destroyed your "Bible in a Year" reading plan?) If people refused to testify and defend the innocent, if they touched anything unclean or were defiled, if they made any rash or foolish vows and then broke them, they were commanded to confess their sin *and then* "bring to the LORD as their penalty a female from the flock, either a sheep or a goat. This will be a sin offering to remove their sin, and the priest will make atonement for them" (v. 6). This is just one of many, many examples from the sacrificial system of how sin, and confession, came at a cost.

Consider Numbers 5. (For those who plowed through Leviticus on a Bible reading plan, Numbers was sure to trip you up.) This passage says: "'Give the following instructions to the people of Israel: If any of the people—men or women—betray the Lord by doing wrong to another person, they are guilty'" (v. 6). Well, that's pretty all-encompassing, right? So what did they have to do? "They must confess their sin [part 1] *and* make full restitution for what they have done [part 2], adding an additional 20 percent and returning it to the person who was wronged" (v. 7, italics mine). This concept was more than just a deterrent from messing with other people's stuff. It was a way of teaching them that sin causes pain beyond the physical damage. Confession wasn't enough to undo the damage. They also had to pay restitution.

Consider Joshua 7. In this chapter, after the miraculous defeat of the mighty city of Jericho, Israel is reeling because they have had their clocks cleaned by the little town of Ai. As they cry out to God to find what has gone wrong, He reveals that someone in the camp has sinned by disobeying His command to completely destroy Jericho and not keep any of the plunder. I find it extremely interesting that God reveals that sin has occurred, but does not reveal the sinner. God knew who had done it, but instead of just pointing out the guilty man to Joshua, He allows them to go through an entire procedure of standing before Joshua and the Lord one family at a time. Why would God do this? Why would God make every family sweat it out when only one person was to blame? I believe God does this so that the entire Israelite nation will experience the weight and the cost of sin and be changed by it. Achan and his family pay the ultimate price, as they are completely destroyed for Achan's sin of hoarding some treasure. While this may seem to us like a high cost for God to expect from them, it would have been completely in keeping with the Jewish understanding of the law and confession.

Consider Ezra 10:11, where Ezra calls the people to "confess your sin to the Lord, the God of your ancestors, *and do* what he demands. Separate yourselves from the people of the land and from these pagan women" (italics mine). Confession was part one; changing their ways was part two.

Consider Proverbs 28:13: "People who conceal their sins will not prosper, but if they confess and turn from them, they will receive mercy."

Consider Acts 19:18-19: "Many who became believers confessed their sinful practices. A number of them who had been practicing sorcery brought their incantation books and burned them at a public bonfire. The value of the books was several million dollars." Confession led to action.

And finally, consider 2 Corinthians 5:21 and the cross of Jesus Christ. Though He had nothing to confess, "For God made Christ, who never sinned, to be the offering for our sin, so that we could be made right with God through Christ." When we confess, we are claiming the blood of Christ as covering for our sin. This is the highest cost imaginable, is it not?

But therein lies the danger. Because the ultimate price has already been paid for our sin through the cross of Christ, we are prone to lose sight of this important connection between confession and restitution. Sin still costs something; it cost Jesus His life for us. And when we confess, we need to enter into a mindset that confession comes with change. This is the second half of the equation. Confession by itself does not produce life change. Confession *plus* repentance—taking steps toward restitution and turning away from our sin—equals freedom.

This, my friends, is the New Testament concept of repentance. To repent is to confess *and then* to turn away from what we have been doing or worshipping or idolizing. Confession is our job. We are called—no, even commanded—to confess our sins. We must choose this. But the restitution for sin, the turning away from sin requires help. It always has. The "and then" of repentance is where others come in and is a topic we will turn to the chiastic flip of this one, Chapter 8.

OUR STORY: BUT I DON'T WANT TO!

So there it is. The both/and of our confession. On the one hand, confession is the starting place of everything. Confession is the decision to get real about the places we have worked so hard to hide. Confession is open rebellion against "church nice" and "doing fine" culture. Confession is to acknowledge that things are not always as they seem, and it is the beginning of our healing. Most importantly, confession enables us to finally experience the kind of community that does transform us. Dietrich Bonhoeffer, a German theologian who was killed under the Hitler regime, says it well: "The final breakthrough to fellowship does not occur, because, though they have fellowship with one another as believers and as devout people, they do not have fellowship as the undevout, as sinners. The pious fellowship permits no one to be a sinner. So everyone must conceal his sin from himself and the fellowship. The fact is that we are sinners."[6] To confess is to finally and truly join a fellowship, not of the pious, but of the sinner-saints who have been saved by grace.

On the other hand, confession is not the end-all and it is not enough to bring lasting freedom. When we are trapped in sin, we can live with an idea that goes like this, "If I just get it out in the open, I will be free." In this ideal, we actually end up making an idol of confession. Confession does not set us free; Jesus alone can do that. Confession is what puts us in the starting blocks for what Jesus most wants to do in our life: bring lasting change. Lasting change is the result of new patterns, new decisions, and new community experienced over time.

By this point in the chapter, I can hear an objection that you might be raising. Simply put, you are saying, "I don't want to do this!" If you are willing to be honest, in your heart of hearts you don't want to confess. You don't want to be fully aware of what you have done and the impact it can have on others. You don't want to revisit some of those places your mind has built a steel fortress around in order to protect. Hiding is hard, but confessing sounds infinitely more challenging and messy. Are you honest enough to say that you feel this way? Good! Because all of us have lived there. We don't confess because we want to or we feel like it; we confess because we need to and because we believe that it is the starting gate of freedom. Believe me, though, I understand; you have good reasons not to confess. Some of your reasons might include these:

MY CONFESSION WILL HURT OTHER PEOPLE

This reason almost sounds noble. You feel that not confessing and instead holding the truth inside is the more loving thing to do. If your wife knew of your indiscretions, small or large, it would hurt her very much. If your boss or coworkers knew what you had done behind their backs, they might feel violated or deceived. If your small group knew what you'd been hiding, it could create fear and bring disunity to the group. *Isn't hiding my sin worth it,* you think, *if I can spare others all of this discomfort and pain?*

The truth is, you have already done the thing that would hurt others. Confessing isn't what will hurt; what hurts is the truth of what you've done. And the reality is that by not telling others, the situation is getting worse. Don't believe me? Answer these questions:

- Does hiding a behavior cause you to be more or less shallow, quick to judge, and angry in your relationships?

- Does keeping a secret make you want to, at times, withdraw and isolate from those you love?

- And the best one: Does hiding the truth make it more or less likely that you will do the thing again?

When we are willing to start asking (and answering) questions like these, our objection that confession will hurt others starts to fall apart. *Not* confessing will hurt others far more than confessing ever will.

MY CONFESSION WILL HURT ME

Ah, now that's a little more honest, isn't it? Even if you say that your confession could hurt others, aren't you really most afraid of the cost it could have for you? Confessing your sexual sin could cause a serious fracture in your marriage or dating relationship. To repair this wound could, and likely will, take years. Confessing your behaviors at work could have costly implications to your hours or even your position in the company. You may be asked to step down from positions, step off teams, and step out of roles that you have held for many years. With all this at stake, why take the risk? Why not just carry it?

Facing this pain is actually part of your restitution; this is the process of learning that sin has a cost, and it is this lesson that will begin to change you. I want to say this in love, but as bluntly as possible: You need to face the music for your actions, and the sooner the better. The longer you go in secrecy, the more opportunity you give Satan to create havoc in your life. Never forget that the enemy has come to steal, kill, and destroy, and when you hold onto unconfessed areas of your life, you leave that part of your life wide open to his schemes.

Here's the truth that you know instinctively: It is always better when confession comes on our terms and at the time of our own choosing. Even the public law of our land will deal more leniently with someone who chooses to confess their guilt. How much more will people who love and care about you be empowered to act on your behalf if you make the choice to self-disclose?

Unfortunately, the alternative is seen far too often. Rather than choosing to confess, people hide out until they are caught and then it gets nasty. Marriages end, pastors are fired, jobs are taken away, credibility is gone. Forced disclosure as a result of being found out is never pretty. Jesus promised us, "For the time is coming when everything that is covered will be revealed, and all that is secret will be made known to all" (Matthew 10:26). The way I see it, everything we have done and are currently doing will one day be brought to light, if not in this world, then before the very throne of God Himself. We can choose either to bring things to light now or later. We can choose a little bit of pain and discomfort now, or a lot of pain and discomfort later. Choosing now means the opportunity to discover grace and change in this life and with the people God has given us on this journey.

MY CONFESSION WILL PUSH OTHERS AWAY

If you have lived with secrets for a long time, you may believe a lie that has become a normal part of the fabric of your life. From childhood, you have listened to a voice that says, *If they knew about _____, they would reject me! If they knew about _____, they wouldn't like me, they wouldn't marry me, they wouldn't want to be with me.* This belief says people will reject the real me. *The hidden me is ugly, twisted, and sick,* you think. *Why on earth would I expose others to that?*

The truth that I have found over and over is that when I choose to be honest and real, people do not run away. There may be exceptions. Some may find the truth to be too hard to bear and they will walk away, but I want to suggest that this is not the most common reaction by any means. In fact, the exact opposite has proved to be true in my own life and in the lives of other men with whom I have worked. When I humble myself and choose to confess my sin, people actually draw near to me. The truth may be painful and confession may cause some long conversations and a long process of restoring trust, but this choice has always created deeper, stronger relationships.

One of the truths you will discover in confession is that people weren't as snookered by the projected self as you thought. When you open up, people get to see the real person they have longed to meet and know all along. When we live in secrets, we already fear that people will reject us, and so we live in this kind of half-life where all our relationships are only half-real. Confession is a bold decision to wake up and be fully alive with others. Is it unnerving and fear inducing? Well sure. But it is transforming!

When we open up our lives, we also give others permission to do the same. We expose our weaknesses and our humanity, and so others decide they can do the same. In a similar fashion, when we project a false self who has it all together, people around us instinctively know to do likewise. This is one of the most unfortunate outcomes of playing "church nice." We all sit together in a room and long to be truly known, but instead we stay covered up. But when somebody plunges in and gets real, others will always follow. Don't listen to the lie for a moment that says others would reject the real you. They might not necessarily enjoy your sin, but they long to have fellowship with you in the wonderful journey of being transformed from honest places of sin and brokenness to places of God's redemption and freedom.

WHAT ABOUT ACCOUNTABILITY?

Another way you may want to push back by now is to say, "Well, what about accountability? Isn't that the other half of confession? We confess to trusted brothers or sisters, and then we ask them to keep us accountable not to do it again." This idea of an accountability group is common in Christianity. I experienced accountability groups at several different junctures in my life. Let me tell you briefly about one of those and why I think it was an epic failure, even though I loved the group and each of the men dearly.

One of my early experiences of confession was to a good friend in college. We had begun meeting weekly to pray and encourage one another. After about three months of this, I got honest enough to admit my struggle with pornography, and so did he. Within a few weeks, there were four of us who met weekly to pray, encourage one another, and hold each other accountable to not view pornography or masturbate. We sincerely wanted God's purity in our lives. For a time, this worked incredibly well for me; I was pure for a couple of months. When the behavior crept back into my life, I had to drag myself into a group meeting and confess—again—that I had blown it. Like most accountability groups, these guys were supportive and affirming. "We believe in you. You'll beat this. God will strengthen you." They said all the right things and they prayed for me with true faith that God would set me free.

And so a pattern began. I would walk in a time of freedom, only to act out again. This would cause the predictable shame and guilt, which I would hide for a brief time. Then I would confess, shed a few tears, and walk in a time of freedom. Maybe a day, maybe a week, maybe a month, but it always happened again. Wash, rinse, repeat. I found that I actually became comfortable in sharing with these guys. On the one hand, it was good to know there was grace, but on the other hand it was all too convenient to stay unchanged.

What this group became for me—and I think this is the experience for many men—was one more place I was trying to perform. Each week, we'd go around and ask, "How was your week? Did you mess up again?" To say "no" was an achievement and made me feel good. To say "yes" was failure and a decision to redouble my efforts at purity and try harder the next week. What I discovered is that I had patterns of behavior that were more powerful than my ability to believe and perform them away. I couldn't "want" the change bad enough to make it happen.

Allow me to illustrate this from the world of sports. I once ran a half marathon (13.1 miles) that took place not more than six blocks from my house. It's a rare thing in running to compete on your "home course" and I couldn't pass up the opportunity. I also knew that this race had a very small field of runners, and as someone who stayed in good shape and pushed myself hard, I knew I had a real shot at coming in first. I have been running for twelve years and never sniffed anything close to first place overall. Visions of grandeur filled my dreams the night before.

As the race began, the lead pack quickly dwindled to just two of us. I looked over and saw a young high school kid jogging along with me. I secretly hoped that he was just a naive teen who didn't really know how long the race was and that when we hit the challenging hills a couple miles in, he would fade into the distance. But then I got to know him. As we chatted and ran, he started to talk about his track team. I discovered that the night before (less than twelve hours previous), he had competed in a major track meet and finished second in both the mile and the two-mile. He used the words "recovery run" to describe his effort that day. I looked over and noticed that his stride was light, lean, and nimble. I looked down at my own size thirteen feet and felt suddenly heavy and plodding.

By mile eleven, I was beginning to cough and wheeze from the effort. My legs were burning, my lungs were screaming, and my chest was pounding. I looked over at Jack-be-nimble. He was fresh as the morning breeze. I scoured his face for any sign of distress, tiredness or fatigue, or any indication whatsoever that my pace was challenging his conditioning even a little. I saw not even a drop of perspiration. The truth was that this kid was in a whole different league than me. At any given moment, he could have dropped the hammer and scampered off to an easy victory. As it was, he had agreed to tie me for the win, knowing that the prize was a wine gift basket and he was underage. He would get the plaque and I would get the wine, as well as a small shred of my pride still intact.

The point of this story as it relates to our topic is that I couldn't "want" it bad enough to win. I truly desired to win the race, but with the competition running beside me, desire and emotion would not have been enough for me to claim victory. Over the course of a number of years, the elite high school athlete and I had been making thousands of small choices that led us to our current conditioning. He had no doubt logged countless sixty-mile to seventy-mile weeks with speed workouts routinely pushing him to his maximum potential. I had run as well over that time, but I had also spent a lot of time watching football, sitting at a desk, and wrestling with my kids. Because of these repeated behaviors in our lives, we had arrived at two very different places in our capacity.

When it comes to breaking free from places of sexual sin and addiction in our lives, we can't simply desire our way into change. We can't "want" this bad enough to make it happen. An accountability group can be a powerful means to create greater desire for change within us, but that desire alone will not be enough. Our brains have been significantly affected through the years by choices, experiences and relationships. These have created behavioral pathways that we will travel down no matter what promises we have made to others. We cannot perform our way out. But we can train the brain. Accountability groups come up short because they fail to engage the brain on this level.

How do we engage the brain at this level? Sorry for the teaser again, but that will be covered in far greater depth in Chapter 8.

A WORD OF CAUTION

One of the temptations you may feel upon reading some of this material is to head straight to your wife or significant other and come clean with everything. Caution: Don't do that. At least not yet. When we're sick, our tendency is to vomit up everything that's inside of us in order to get it out. We feel better. Lots better. But those around us do not. They get to deal with everything that has come up.

You do need to confess to her. This is not optional. But the way you confess and the timing of it are crucial. For starters, the worst thing you can do is confess to your spouse and then keep on hurting her with the same behavior. Please believe me on this. I did it for a decade with my wife and it caused her intense pain. When you confess, you need to also have the resources, or at least the willingness, to do whatever it takes to change your behavior. I am not saying that you need to be perfect from the point of confession on, but you do need to start rebuilding trust. Trust can only be rebuilt through changed behaviors.

The second worst thing you can do is to confess partially to your wife. When a guy blurts out his sin out of guilt or shame, he will tell his wife a cleaned-up, sanitized version that doesn't really include the depth of his sin. This might make him feel a little better, but it will not accomplish the change that repentance can lead into. And usually, he ends up coming back and telling more of the story, more of the sin, one piece at a time. This is called "staggered disclosure" and the impact it can have on your spouse is the emotional equivalent of the stress faced by a rape victim.[7] That's heavy, I know, but it communicates the high stakes of confessing fully and appropriately.

So what to do? First, you need to go to an advisor, counselor, mentor, or friend that you trust enough to deal maturely with this topic. Pick someone with whom you believe you can be totally and brutally honest. That person can then help you work through disclosing to your wife. The second step is to begin writing out a full history of your behaviors, including specific facts like who, what, and when but without being overly detailed. Writing it out and focusing on the facts will help you speak the truth without justifying it. (For more information on the disclosure process, get the *Seven Pillars of Freedom* workbook from Dr. Ted Roberts and Pure Desire Ministries International.) Third, begin pursuing change. Find a group. Start a group. Visit www.puredesire.org for a list of groups that may meet in your area. Ask your pastor if he knows of any groups. Yes, before you even tell your wife, you need to take steps towards your healing. That way, when the truth comes out, she will see that your confession is already accompanied by action. This is the best way to begin rebuilding the relationship. Finally, read your disclosure statement to your spouse in a time and place where you can process it together in an unhurried, safe environment.

Remember, confession is active rebellion against the unholy desire to look good. So get it all out there and stop looking good. This is the only way you can actually begin to do good.

THE LINCHPIN: THE ETERNAL BOTH/AND

I hope this chapter has given sufficient witness for you to adopt two seemingly contradictory ideas: We must confess in order to experience freedom, and confession will never be enough by itself to establish us in that freedom. Confession is like a skydiver having the courage to step out of the airplane at 20,000 feet. It's crazy, scary, and exhilarating. It may take every ounce of courage and sheer determination we have. We may have to just close our eyes and step. We may even need someone to help push us out. But we must step out in order to change.

As is the case in skydiving, stepping out of the plane isn't nearly as important as what happens next. The experience never starts if we stay in the plane, but if we merely step out and hope to glide easily into change, we are as blind as a skydiver without a parachute and a plan. After confession, we must be ready to fully engage in a process of change. We jump into part two of repentance: the turning away from. This is the eternal both/and of dealing with our sin. Yes, we must confess, *and then* we must devote ourselves fully to transformation. This transformation requires the retraining of our brain, the consistent interaction with other truth-speakers, and a whole lot of God's empowering grace.

One of my all-time favorite verses has to be Colossians 1:29. In this part of the letter, the Apostle Paul has been telling his readers how hard he works to spread the gospel of Jesus Christ. He concludes this part of his letter with the following eye-opening statement: "That's why I work and struggle so hard, depending on Christ's mighty power that works within me." Did you catch the two contradictory ideas? Paul says he works very hard, which might cause us to believe that he was depending on his ability, his skill, and his strength to carry the day when it comes to spreading the gospel. But then Paul says he depended on Christ's mighty power. So which is it? Does Paul think this work is his own, or does he believe this is God's work?

The wonderful answer Paul would give is: Yes. Paul was giving everything he had to do the thing God had called him to do; *at the same time*, he was believing that his only hope for success was God's power. All of Paul, with all of Christ—the one not contradicting or detracting from the other. So also in our recovery it must be the same. All of us. Everything we have to make change happen. But also all of Him. All of His grace, power, and goodness at work in us. When we enter into a life of confession—an ongoing decision to be real about who we were and who we are—we open our lives to all that God has for us. After that, we must be ready to continue to give our all, along with His, to see change happen. This is the eternal both/and. All of Him, all of us, all the time.

> *Dear friends, you always followed my instructions when I was with you. And now that I am away, it is even more important. Work hard to show the results of your salvation, obeying God with deep reverence and fear. For God is working in you, giving you the **desire** and the **power** to do what pleases him.* Philippians 2:12-13 (emphasis added)

CHAPTER FIVE | THE PAIN OF INTIMACY

One of the ironies of sexual sin is how easily we separate it from the real relationships we have. This is very often an outcome of the disconnect we have created between the two sides of ourselves. But healing comes through relationships, primarily with those who are closest to us. Our spouse or significant other will be more affected by this than anyone else, and will have a greater effect on us than anyone else. You may even be reading this book because of the impact your choices have already had on your spouse. So, in our most intimate relationships, we need a deep understanding of the double bind pornography creates. Often, the one who can help us the most (our wife) is the one who is hurt the most. How then, do you navigate this topic with her?

For most of my life, one side of me struggled privately with lust and pornography, while the other side—the public "good" me—learned how to relate to women. These two sides rarely, if ever, spoke to one another. That is, until I was ready to get married. Suddenly and unexpectedly, they collided with great force.

During my sophomore year of college, I began dating my future wife, Michelle. She was awesome in every way—fun, beautiful, smart, athletic, and totally into me! As a lifelong performer, this was more important than I was willing to admit. These early college years, though, were a massive conflict of emotions and behaviors when it came to sexuality. I was involved regularly in my accountability group, but was still relapsing into pornography on a regular basis. Internally, this meant I was a real mess of desires, morality, and spirituality. Externally, I chose to be very careful physically in my relationship with Michelle. Since my hidden behaviors created great doubt in my mind over whether or not I could treat a girl properly in a relationship, I moved slowly. By the standards of our culture, I'm talking slothfully slow. Snails passed me in the fast lane. When my wife and I began dating, I wouldn't even hold her hand for a month. I waited six months for my first kiss. I hesitated for eighteen months before breathing the word "love" into her ear.

Don't mistake me for some "courting only" renaissance kind of guy. Prior to college, I had several other relationships where I quickly told girls I loved them. I hadn't waited at all in previous relationships to hold hands or kiss. Through those early years, I was able to keep my virginity, but I certainly wasn't slow with these girls. So why put on the emergency brake in college? I realized at that time that the stakes were going up; the next girl I dated could very well be the last, and I wanted to do it right. So when I met Michelle, I treated everything physical like a hand grenade with the pin already pulled. I heeded Solomon's words of advice to "not awaken love until the time is right." That was my goal: to keep all my passions and desires, which I feared I couldn't control, asleep for as long as possible.

At the same time that I was making sound, healthy choices relationally, I was continuing to make foolish choices in my mind and my Internet behaviors. While I was in college, the Internet "came of age" and so did my addiction. The free and unlimited access to all kinds of photo libraries proved too great a temptation for me to avoid. These choices, coupled with the budding relationship, left me feeling miserable and conflicted. Here I was, dating the girl of my dreams and making all the right choices with her, while I was shipwrecking my soul and my future behind the scenes.

One of the annual rhythms at our small Christian college was a spiritual-emphasis week with a guest speaker each evening. During our junior year, a guy named David Nassar came and spoke about relationships and encouraged us all to be honest with our future spouse if we were in a serious relationship. He said that we should take time to "air our dirty laundry" with each other prior to the decision to get married. If the other person ran away, we would know it wasn't meant to be. If they heard our worst and were still willing to stay and love us anyway, then we had found someone to whom we could pledge our love for better or for worse.

In my analytical mind, this made total sense. So one night, we drove to a nearby Caribou Coffee (the Midwest rival of Starbucks) and I pulled all the dirty shirts out of my hamper. I told her about childhood experiences, discovering magazines and the Internet, patterns of behavior I'd entered into—everything that I felt was in my closet. It was painful to acknowledge these truths about myself in front of a woman I loved, something I had never done or wanted to do. But this was a significant moment for us.

Though my wife's eyes got large and her voice carried some disbelief, we made it through. She stuck with me. After the lengthy discussion, she asked me a crucial question. "Can't you just promise me," she asked in sincerity and innocence, "that you will never do those things again?" Looking back, I can see that my reply was very typical for someone stuck in denial and self-preservation mode: "I want to, but I know myself too well. I know that no matter how hard I try, it keeps sneaking back in. But I will try harder."

Now, that moment should have been a gigantic flashing red light for me. The woman of my dreams was asking me in love to choose her over my idols of lust and pornography. And I was staring her back in the eye and telling her I didn't have what it took to make that change. Uh, Houston, we have a problem! Sadly, I didn't see the tragic reality of this situation in the moment. I naively believed that my behaviors would simply change over time. I wasn't under any misconception that marriage and sex would fix me, because I had heard enough guys give testimony that this simply wasn't true. But I did think my patterns of sin would just wear themselves out like an old pair of running shoes. I would "wear them out," grow up, and move on. But I didn't.

We married in the summer of 2000. Marriage and sex were great. While we certainly had a learning curve when it came to being physically intimate, our life together was everything I had hoped and dreamed it would be. I was happy. We were happy. Life was grand. But this only highlighted how deeply divided I was. Early in our marriage, I discovered I could be completely satisfied sexually in my wife, and yet hunger for something else. The frequency or fervency of our intimacy had little to no impact on my desire for pornography.

What it did have an impact on was my deep sense of shame. How could I be so well loved, so cared for, so sexually satisfied with my wife, and yet be so ready to run to a cheap substitute? How could I have such a great wife, a great sex life, a great life in general, and jeopardize it all for porn? I felt like a modern-day description of how Esau is described in the book of Hebrews: He sold his birthright for a single bowl of soup. God had given me a whole world of goodness in my wife, and I was sacrificing it all for quick, mental pick-me-ups. I continued to ask, *What is wrong with me?*

What I discovered in marriage is this truth: Pornography is a bigger issue than just wanting sex. This is a lie that pornography feeds us in our youth; we have lots of hormones looking for a way out, and we believe that one day when we enjoy the release through sex, those hormones will be controllable. But this is not the case, because pornography and addiction is really all about feeling good, about filling up a place of pain and emptiness in our brain. No amount of sex or feeling good can fill this hole. Unaware of this, I would fall into porn time and time again, and my shame would increase.

Every so often, I would confess to Michelle. The guilt and shame would build until I couldn't handle the split between who I said I was and what I was doing when no one watched, so I would get honest with my wife. This was always painful. I would make promises, create new boundaries ("I'll never _____ again, I promise!"), and be "fixed" for a while. But this "confession without turning away from" (see Chapter 4) meant I always turned back. It seems like I discovered hundreds of different ways to fall into sin because it was never exactly the same way twice. The boundaries would work to an extent, but I would always find a new way around them.

I also had seasons where I wouldn't confess. I would try to just keep it in and deal with it between God and myself. This may have been even more painful because of how the shame increased and the lies persisted. "Look how good your wife is being to you, and look at what you're doing behind her back! If she knew, she would hate you. She would leave you." I was so close to her and so uncomfortable around her. I felt more divided around her than around anyone else in all my life. The one who was supposed to know me best, I felt really knew me least of all. I hated hiding, but I didn't know what else to do. Kind of like a couple in the Bible.

GOD'S STORY: WE WERE NAKED...AND ASHAMED

Let's be honest. As churches, we're not so good at talking about sex. It seems like the topic either gets avoided or else tossed around as a publicity stunt to get more people in church, like a church in Texas that encouraged its members to have sex every night for forty days. Even churches aren't above the capitalist truth that sex sells. Because of this hot or cold approach to sexuality, some passages don't get the fair and honest treatment that they should, or else they get softened so as not to be too edgy.

Look at Genesis 3. We have turned this story of the fall of man into a nice children's tale about apples and snakes, when in truth the story wraps itself around the themes of nudity and shame.

The story of Genesis 3 actually begins in Genesis 2:25. Remember, God didn't put in the chapter divisions and verse numbers. The author of the book didn't take the time to carefully divide the stories for us; all of these decisions were made much later. These artificial divisions can, at times, cause us to miss a verse or thought that really helps define the passage. Such is the case in our Genesis story. Genesis 2:25, the proper introduction to Genesis 3, reads, "Now the man and his wife were both naked, but they felt no shame."

Think about that. Adam and Eve were in God's perfectly created world, as God's uniquely made creation, enjoying God's freely given gift of one another. And they were naked with no shame. In my youth, I always thought this verse indicated that they loved and accepted one another so completely, that they didn't need to hide their physical bodies. Others taught me that the hope of a good marriage was to completely accept my spouse just the way she was, so that I could also feel "naked and unashamed." But do you realize that this is actually a very post-fall way of reading back into these verses? Adam and Eve would never have understood that line of thinking.

Picture their scenario pre-fall. Their physical bodies were perfect in every way. No disease had touched the world, no sickness had diminished them, and they held no competing views of beauty with other people. Apart from a slight scar on Adam's side for the rib God had used in creating Eve, their bodies were as pure, natural, and unblemished as possible. The lack of shame that Adam and Eve felt toward one another was not about the acceptance of one another's physical bodies. They felt no shame because they had absolutely nothing to hide. Adam and Eve experienced complete intimacy with one another and with God. Intimacy, true intimacy, is the opposite of shame. Intimacy is the complete and unhindered knowledge of another person. Shame is the desire to cover up so that another's knowledge of us is incomplete. Shame and intimacy cannot coexist because shame blocks us from experiencing true intimacy.

This was the state of Adam and Eve's nudity. They were intimate in every possible sense of the word—physically, emotionally, and spiritually. Into this picture, Satan comes slithering along. His objective is to destroy this perfect intimacy. His desire wasn't so much about getting them to "sin" per se; his primary aim was to break the perfect relationship they had with God and one another. Satan's fall from Heaven had involved that same breaking of intimate fellowship with the Father, and he has been hell-bent on destroying intimacy between God and humans ever since.

So the serpent hissed to Eve, "Did God say you must not eat any of the fruit in the garden?" I love the way the New Living Translation treats the first spoken word of Satan: "Really?" (It helps if you read that word with the scoffing, incredulous tone of a teenage boy.) His initial word was to sow doubt that God could be trusted. The serpent wanted to plant the idea in Eve's mind that God had in some way been false with them. This is such a huge point because if God had been false, then the intimacy Adam and Eve had enjoyed with God was undermined. The intimacy is lessened if God had been untruthful, or "covered," toward them.

At first, Eve refuted this attempt by the serpent as she quoted back God's command to them regarding the trees. Again, Satan's reply was to doubt God's word to them, "You won't die! God knows that your eyes will be opened when you eat it. You will become just like God, knowing everything, both good and evil." Now Satan was being more direct to question God's word. He was trying to convince Eve that God had purposefully held out on them. If this were the case, then God could not be trusted at all. Mike Wilkerson put it this way in his book, *Redemption*: "But the Serpent's story cast a shadow on their experience and offered to interpret their [already perfect] lives by lies: Something is missing. God withholds his best. Why should you be satisfied living under God, when you could live as god?"[8] In other words, there's something better out there than the intimacy you are currently enjoying with God in His plan.

Eve takes the bait. The Bible says, "The woman was convinced." Convinced of what? Convinced that God hadn't told them everything and that a better way of doing life existed (eating the fruit) from the way God had given them (not eating the fruit). Just as the serpent had promised, their eyes were opened the moment they ate—only with a much different result than expected. This is a common result of sin. We get whatever is promised us, but that promise looks and feels much different than we expected it would. When their eyes were opened, what's the first thing they noticed? Their nudity. They were naked. Almost makes it sound like they didn't realize they were unclothed.

But look again. The issue here isn't that they were in the buff. The real issue is that they *felt shame* over their nakedness. They were not surprised by the nudity; they were surprised that being nude with one another suddenly felt wrong. Why on earth is that? Had their bodies changed? Had they suddenly grown old and wrinkled and feared the other's reaction? No. The truth is that they now had something to hide. And whenever we have something to hide, it affects our whole self—body, mind, and soul. What they had to hide wasn't even between the two of them. They were both implicit in this plot, but they now had something to hide from God. This knowledge also separated them from one another.

Wow! Think through the significance of that! Now we are starting to understand the deep implications of our sin. At this time in the story, God showed up. They heard Him walking in the garden, indicating that they were familiar with the sound of His approach. For the first time ever, they hated the way His presence made them feel. They usually looked forward to His coming and strolling through the garden with Him. They had been relaxed, free, and easy in His presence.

But not this time. This time, His coming provoked great fear, and so they hid. They didn't want to, but they didn't know what else to do. The presence of the One who knew them best created a deep feeling of shame. He doesn't know everything about them anymore and suddenly they have something to cover up. And so, they literally hide. They hid parts of their bodies behind fig leaves, and they hid their whole selves behind bushes; anything they could do to keep from being seen by the One who sees all things. What a foolish idea! That we could hide from the God of the universe. They tried it then, and we still attempt it all the time, don't we?

God seems to play along with their ruse. He called out, "Where are you?" Don't think for a moment that He was truly confused or confounded by their duplicity. He asked where they were in order to give them the opportunity to disclose, to confess. And Adam did. He didn't answer the question God asked, but he did answer the deeper question being suggested, not "where" but "why." Why did you hide? Adam cried out, "I heard you, so I hid. I was afraid because I was naked."

Did you catch the unbelievable truth expressed there? Adam doesn't hide because he is naked, but because he is *afraid*. He is afraid that God will truly see him for who he is; for the first time ever, that thought frightened Adam. He was frightened because he had something to hide and he was fearful of how God would react. Shame always produces the need to hide our true self for fear of the rejection or pain that being discovered will cause. We experience this most deeply with God, but are often unaware that we are feeling it with God; we experience this feeling more commonly with other people, particularly with the one we are closest to, our spouse. Adam was suddenly uncomfortably close with God. We are uncomfortably close with one another.

God then asks Adam an interesting question. "Who told you that you were naked?" In other words, God wants to know where Adam got the idea that he had something to hide. God goes on to ask, "Have you eaten the fruit I commanded you not to eat?"

You see, there is only one place that sends us the message we have something to hide: our sin. Sin is any decision to do something other than what God has asked, and in so doing we are diminished because we become less than what God intended. Sin leads us to believe there is something wrong with us. Our eyes are opened and we feel shame at who we are. We are naked and ashamed. When we feel this way—that we are less than God intended—we hide from God and others, out of fear.

The Genesis 3 story concludes with some blaming and then God cursed the serpent as well as Adam and Eve, banishing them from the garden. All these are interesting parts of the story, but not relevant to our current discussion. What is relevant is one final detail toward the end of the story, as Adam and Eve are being ushered out of the garden. Almost as an aside, Genesis 3:21 states, "And the LORD God made clothing from animal skins for Adam and his wife." You know what this is? This is a loving God covering over the shame of His people. This is God declaring, "I see you; I love you; and I am going to cover over your shame. You don't have to hide anymore." God has been giving us a covering ever since.

The activity of God in covering us forms holy bookends on the entire Jewish sacrificial system. The first ever sacrifice is made by God here in Genesis 3 when He took one of His perfect creations and destroyed it in order to cover over the shame of Adam and Eve. And the final sacrifice is also made by God some four millennia later, when He took the perfect Son and destroyed Him on the cross for you and me. God began the sacrificial system, and He concluded it. Through Jesus Christ, He declares, "I have covered your shame. Do not be afraid." For us, Jesus is the end of our shame. Friends, the time has come for us to step out of hiding and be known by God. In so doing, we can finally be known and experience true intimacy with others.

OUR STORY: NAKED AND UNASHAMED

I have run several marathons in my life, but one that I have never entered is Grandma's Marathon in Duluth, Minnesota. You may be surprised to hear that this is one of the most popular marathons in the country, with a registration cap of ten thousand typically filling up in a few days. The marathon is popular because of the general downhill descent of the course from the start in the hill country around Duluth to the finish in downtown. Because of this course layout, I am told that participants can see the finish line area from as far out as fifteen miles! To me, this would be incredibly disheartening. Running a marathon is hard enough without the finish line, still miles away, taunting you from a great distance. My heart would shout, "That's where I want to be!" while my legs would protest, "But we'll never get there!"

This may be how you feel about true intimacy. Somewhere in your heart, you long for this place of being fully and freely known by others. But another part of you screams out that the journey is too far and too painful, so why even bother. The purpose of this chapter is to help you see why true intimacy is so difficult and recognize that your closest relationships might be the most painful. I hope you might also see why you might be avoiding God. Shame has a way of separating us from those who can help us. I am heading toward some solutions to this problem, but I want you to first see how shame operates in your life today. I hope all along in these pages, you will find yourself exclaiming, "So *that's* what has been going on. Finally, I understand!" Understanding the cycle is the birthplace of changing it.

We are separated from God and others by shame. Shame is different than guilt. Guilt is a God-given response to our negative behaviors that says to our heart or our conscience, "What I did was wrong." Guilt enables us to identify behaviors and patterns that need to be dealt with in the context of relationships. Shame, however, goes far beyond guilt. Shame says, "Who I am is wrong." Rather than identifying behaviors or patterns as bad, we look inside and conclude that we are bad. If we are essentially a good person who does bad things, we can confess and deal with those things. But if we are essentially a bad person who can't help but also do bad things, then we must cover up and hide. What other choice do we have?

This puts us on the **Shame Cycle**, as illustrated below.

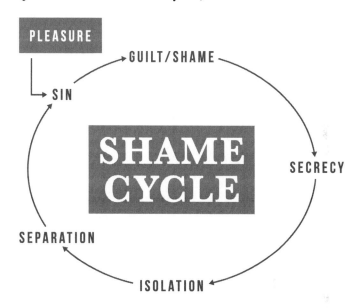

As human beings, we desire to experience pleasure. This pleasure can be of the highest form by following God and doing His will, or it can be of the very lowest form where we give in to the serpent's lies. We believe that a better way exists than what God has provided. The book of James in the Bible puts it this way: "Temptation comes from our own desires, which entice us and drag us away. These desires give birth to sinful actions. And when sin is allowed to grow, it gives birth to death" (James 1:14-15). Anytime we make this choice to give in to our base desires for pleasure, we head down the path toward death.

Sin creates a sense of shame or guilt about what we have done: *shame* if we believe we are bad, or *guilt* if we believe that only our behavior was bad. In either case, the shame and guilt puts us in an awkward place. We have to deal with it in one way or another. To face ourselves and our behavior in the presence of God and others would be painful. We can see the pain ahead of us on that path. In the shame cycle, we choose to avoid pain. Do you realize that most, if not all, of your addictive, negative behavior is fueled by a desire to avoid pain? We live at a time when the concept of healthy or redemptive pain has disappeared almost entirely, so it makes perfect sense that we would be programmed to choose against it. But choosing to avoid pain launches us deeper into the Shame Cycle.

If we choose to avoid the pain that facing ourselves and our actions would cause, then we have no other choice but Secrecy. We hide what we have done, or who we are, from the view of others. And let me emphasize: We cannot hide from others without also hiding from God. We deceive ourselves if we think we can keep it from others, but be totally honest with God. I know this might be a complete contradiction from the way you have handled sin and confession up until now, but believe me when I say it's true. I will explain more later.

Whenever we choose Secrecy, this creates Isolation. We have covered over a part of our lives, and this puts a distance between ourselves and others. Isolation is primarily emotional and mental—a decision that I must guard who I truly am from your view. Isolation will always create Separation.

Separation is distance, either physical or relational, between us and God and others. This is the "death" spoken of in James 1. We don't have to kick the bucket to start experiencing this kind of death because whenever we live separated from God and those we love, we are tasting death already. We are hiding behind the bushes because we are afraid. The Pure Desire Ministries workbook, *Seven Pillars of Freedom*, explains the process this way: "Sin that has not been dealt with leads to shame that drives us to secrecy (hiding). The consequence of this sequence is that secrecy always creates isolation and the isolation always leads to separation."[9] This is the shame cycle that catches us in its claws and fights to keep us for life.

The saddest reality might be that this is indeed a *cycle*. This is not only a one-way street that we head down when we choose sin and secrecy. Every time we choose this path, we make it more likely that we will go down it again. And again. And again. Why? Because when we are separated from community with others and from communion with God, sin is always right at our doorstep. Avoiding sin through personal effort in isolation is always a doomed endeavor. This is why I confessed to my wife for a decade in our marriage without changing. I was caught in the shame cycle, trying harder and harder to do what was right, but always on my own.

The Shame Cycle will leave you like it left me, uncomfortably close in your marriage, and in other core relationships. The closer you are to someone and the more you desire to be loved by them, the greater your need will be to protect and cover up weaknesses and shame out of fear of pain or rejection. So with those you know the *best*, you are actually pretending the *most*. And this is a rotten place to be.

This will lead you in one of two directions. The first direction is to begin shifting blame away from yourself and onto those closest to you. And the longer you stay in the Shame Cycle, the more you will do it. Why? Because you are programming your brain to avoid pain. The sense of shame you carry is so painful that you must find ways to deal with it. The easiest way to deal with the pain is to cast it off on someone else, believing that "they make me feel this way." In an effort to make yourself feel better, you will push away the person most equipped to help.

The second, and more common, direction you can head is to accept a life of false intimacy. False intimacy occurs when you purposefully choose how much of yourself to reveal—usually just enough to create a sense of truth, but not so much as to make it reflect negatively on yourself. You are partially known, but not fully so. Sadly, this kind of false intimacy is what characterizes the vast majority of relationships I see today. Couples become so accustomed to half-baked intimacy that the real thing remains out of reach.

Adam and Eve lived in uncomfortable closeness with their Creator after the Fall. And we have felt the need to hide ever since, getting trapped over and over on the Shame Cycle. I spun on it myself for more than a decade, feeling awkwardly close to God and my wife. But Jesus has a way of spinning us out. His death, when we fully embrace its significance on a personal level, does far more than merely cover our shame. Our shame became His shame so that we might experience the righteousness of God. Living in this new righteousness is the subject of the next few chapters.

A WORD ON FALSE INTIMACY

One of the most unfortunate outcomes of a sex-driven culture is the equating of sex with intimacy. Certainly, intimacy in a marriage includes sex, and sex can be intimate, but sex does not equal intimacy. As I have talked about intimacy in this chapter, some readers may have been confused and objected, thinking, *Hey, wait a minute! We don't struggle with intimacy. We have sex all the time. We are very intimate.* But sex is not the same as intimacy, no matter how hard our culture tries to substitute the one for the other. Unable to experience true intimacy, we sell out for a false sense of intimacy created through sex. In the words of my friend Dr. Ted Roberts: "Welcome to crazy." The thing we want most (intimacy) we don't know how to get, so we keep running after the one thing (sex) we think will bring what we want most.

The fact is that sex in many marriages and relationships is often a cover-up for a lack of true intimacy. This is a poor substitute. Sex in this manner reduces intimacy to a passion, an emotion, and a feeling. And when we have reduced intimacy to this definition, then it is possible to experience "intimacy" in all kinds of ways and with many different people.

The model for intimacy, though, is not Hollywood or adult films; the model for intimacy is the Trinity. God exists in Himself as a perfect unity of three in complete knowledge of one another. The three persons of the Trinity are so complete in their knowledge of one another and so "uncovered" in the presence of each other that the three are actually said to be one. We are to model our pursuit of intimacy after this perfect display of God in unity with Himself.

Before you object and say, "But how can we be like the Trinity?" remember what God says in Genesis 2:24 where He lays out the pattern for us: "This explains why a man leaves his father and mother and is joined to his wife, and *the two are united into one*" (italics mine). A man and a wife can live together in such perfect intimacy that the two people are actually described as one. This is the image of the Trinity in us.

And do you know what the very next verse in Genesis 2 is? You guessed it: "Now the man and his wife were both naked, but they felt no shame" (Genesis 2:25). That is intimacy.

THE LINCHPIN

Intimacy is the result of being known in all the brutal honesty and uncovered truth about ourselves and finding that even there, we are loved still. We cannot experience true intimacy without honesty and truth. This is an issue of trust. As author John Lynch puts it, we are learning to "trust God and others with who we really are."[10] This is the beginning of freedom: As we open the depths of who we are to God and others, we find that they do not run away in shock and horror. In fact, when we step out in trust by choosing honesty and truth, we find that others actually move toward us.

How do we get to that place of trust? We must go back to the point where Adam and Eve missed it. They fell into sin because they gave in to the lie that God had held out on them—that a better life existed than the one God promised. Trust is the process of coming before God day after day and affirming, "The best life possible is the one You have given me to live. Teach me to live in it with grace, confidence, and joy." In making this decision—that God alone holds the keys to our best life—we can then have enough confidence to open up who we really are.

When we know that God has something great for us, and He really does, we can face the pain of who we are, or believe we are, in order to get to that destination. Will all of our sin just go away or change overnight? No. But as Lynch goes on to say, "The goal is not for you to get all of your 'stuff' solved. You never will. There is an endless list of stuff. God is gracious to reveal only a snippet at a time. The goal is to learn to depend on— to trust—what God says is true about you, so that together you can begin dealing with that stuff."[11] Learning to depend on what God says is true about you. I like that. We can never hear what God says is true about us, though, until we face the lies of the serpent and replace them with God's truth. Living in that truth may seem a long ways off, but you can get there. Will the journey be long? Sure. Will there be pain to encounter. You bet. Will it be worth it? Without a doubt! Let's find out how this journey takes off in the next chapter.

O LORD, you have examined my heart and know everything about me. You know when I sit down or stand up. You know my thoughts even when I'm far away... You go before me and follow me. You place your hand of blessing on my head. Such knowledge is too wonderful for me, too great for me to understand! Psalm 139:1-2, 5-6

PART 2: THE BREAKTHROUGH PEAK

CHAPTER SIX | BROKEN IN ALL THE RIGHT PLACES

One of the highlights of my summers as a teen was a week-long backpacking trip into various mountain ranges around the beautiful state of Montana. My dad had a passion for the outdoors, for camps, and for teens, and so he had launched a backpacking ministry in Wyoming and brought it with him to Montana after we moved.

One of my favorite experiences on these trips was a midweek summit of the highest peak accessible within the vicinity of our base camp. Something about sitting on a high mountain peak and surveying the world around me captured my heart and my imagination. A perspective and a peace settle into my soul at ten thousand feet of elevation that is hard to explain or define back in my day-to-day living.

During one trip, we were camped in the Crazy Mountain range near Bozeman. The summit of our choosing was Sunlight Peak, a barren mound of rock that dominated the landscape around it. The hike began routinely enough in the lowlands as we made our way through grassy meadows toward the true ascent. When we neared the last one thousand-foot climb, which required scrambling around several rock ledges, a negative weather pattern developed. We were hiking with an experienced guide, though, who felt confident this was only a brief, passing storm. He believed we could continue if we took our time and climbed with care. Keep in mind, however, that on a previous trip this same guide had looked up into a cloudy sky and commented, "Looks like a ten-minute storm to me." Three days later—when the rain stopped—his weather prediction skills were in serious doubt. So hearing him forecast a "passing storm" did little to calm my fears.

Based on this assessment, however, our guide continued to lead us on a careful ascent up the last leg of the trail. You should know I have a mild fear of heights, and so ascending a peak is a bit of a mental challenge to begin with. But as those clouds rolled in and the peak fogged over, I found the panic in me beginning to rise. A few minutes later, the wind picked up and rain began to splatter the bare rock to which I was now clinging. As I looked down several thousand feet to the valley floor below, I wondered if I had lost my mind. Reaching the peak would be a nice accomplishment, but that notch on my belt was little consolation compared to the possibility of slipping and plummeting to my death. But I was no quitter, so I kept with the group and continued this treacherous ascent.

My friends, we are on a similar journey. In this book, I have described a path through life that is at times dark, treacherous, and filled with peril. We have ascended through birth and childhood, where we took on messages about our identity and our sexuality. We learned to cope in our teenage years and developed patterns of acting out in order to feel good, and some of those patterns continue to this day. We have struggled through honesty, confession, and the pain of intimacy. By this point on the trip, you may be feeling like I did that day clinging to the rocks of Sunlight Peak so many years ago. The summit may feel very far away and the path to it cloudy and uncertain. Perhaps you're also feeling this journey is hardly worth the pain or the risk or the possible failure. But let me take a moment and assure you that everything we have packed through thus far has prepared us for this moment. Breakthrough Peak. The sun is going to emerge and everything will take on a new form in your life. It certainly did in mine. If you find yourself beginning to grow disillusioned with the journey, take heart. You are nearly there. And once you are, the perspective gained from the summit will put everything else into a welcome perspective. What may seem like a dark path blanketed in storm clouds now will one day be the road you look back on with great joy.

By the winter of 2010, my wife and I had been on a ten-year roller coaster with pornography. My seemingly endless cycle of binge-purge-confess-repeat was weighing down our entire relationship. We had reached a breaking point when it came to my addiction. Something had to give. No matter how much I confessed, and no matter how many boundaries or consequences we put in place, I would end up back in the mud again. By this point in our marriage, I was confessing every time I relapsed. In a sense, I was sinning less, as my forays into pornography were briefer and lighter, but the pain it was causing was growing worse for my wife because I was being more honest. I had a relapse in January of that year, and for the first time a shocking truth hit me: My wife could leave me over this. This was a new idea to my denial-soaked brain. I had worked so hard convincing myself, and her, that this problem had nothing to do with her that I was unwilling to open my eyes to the true impact it was having on her.

Though this fall was similar to many that had occurred before, something was different in her reaction this time. In the past, I had been aware of her pain, but excused it with the thought, *If she just understood this problem, she wouldn't be so hurt by it.* The impetus for change was on her; if she matured in her view of my struggle, she could be more supportive and quit making the issue about her. Boy, was I messed up in my thinking! When she looked at me with that pain in her eyes, the pain that said, "I don't know how to be around you anymore," the tables turned and I realized that I was the one who did not understand. My actions that I thought of as "just porn" and "a guy thing" were destroying my marriage. This could not go on any longer. Now the impetus for change was squarely on my shoulders. I knew that if this happened again, I could lose her. She would leave, not because she hated me and couldn't stand me, but because the pain was so great that she wouldn't know how to stay. And I would have no excuse. She would be justified in leaving in order to find a way to deal with the pain.

As in the past, I followed up on this failure the way I knew best. I redoubled my personal change efforts. I tried harder. I strengthened and elevated all my boundaries. I made promises and put a deeper focus on my spiritual life—all good steps, but all of them insufficient to bring change. In February of that year, I was away from home on a trip, taking a week-long class. After a particularly mentally taxing day, and one in which I had received some stressful news about a couple in the church back home, I was physically and emotionally drained. I knew from experience that this was a personal "danger zone" when it came to pornography. Something in my heart whispered that I should not be alone even for a moment.

But by the end of the day, there I was: by myself, isolated, in a room with my computer. And all my desires, promises, and boundaries were not enough in that moment to keep me pure. I ran back to the mistress that had supported me at times like this since I was fifteen years old. The pattern I had learned so well kicked into gear and I did what I had trained my brain to do.

In that moment, God gave me the first of two incredible gifts: pain. Pain that was almost unbearable. I saw myself, as if in a mirror, for the first time. How could I have done this again? I had foreseen the danger and knew I was vulnerable. I even believed that if I stumbled again, my wife would leave me. If my wife left, I felt certain I would lose my job as a pastor. And even with all of this at play in my mind, I still did the very thing I had promised myself not to do. I echoed the words of the Apostle Paul in Romans 7, "Oh, what a miserable person I am! Who will free me from this life that is dominated by sin?"

This moment caused a pain deep in my heart. I had never hurt like this over my addiction. I hurt for my wife. I hurt for the pain telling the truth would cause—and I knew immediately that I had to tell her. I hurt for the fact that I didn't know how to change; this behavior was bigger than my ability to handle it. For me, this was the hardest admission of all. In my mind, I could handle anything. If you asked my friends or family, they would say I have a way of making things work and making life work out in my favor. I thrived under pressure and stress. I endured through difficult circumstances. I believed there was no problem too big that I couldn't study, lead, or work my way through. Until that moment.

Someone has said that we never change until the pain of staying the same is greater than the pain of changing. Indeed, pain has a way of changing us, and the pain I felt that night opened me up to change in a new way. I finally believed that I didn't have what it took to change my life. I was finally broken in my pride and self-sufficiency. I wrote in a letter to myself that night these words: "I cannot trust myself. I am dangerous when I am alone, and the pain is unbelievably deep. Why can't

I remember how this feels? I am not a good person when I am alone, unless I am consciously focused on something else. I don't build in enough safeguards. I need to make serious change...." My heart was crying out for something, but I honestly didn't know where to turn.

As hard as it was, I faced the truth and told my wife. Together, we began to make some changes. The first step was to give away the keys to my choices. With my wife's help, we established a new pattern of life that included pretty radical boundaries for me: no visiting sports websites online, no watching TV alone, no entering bookstores or gas stations alone—all of these and more were aimed at eliminating my danger zones. The boundaries I had set for myself in the past were like knee-high barricades I could leap over with ease, but these new boundaries felt like ten-foot high stone walls guarded by an angry lion.

But even then, I felt like I was merely holding on for dear life. Dr. Ted Roberts calls it "white-knuckling" life; we use every ounce of strength we have to just keep the car on the road and right side up. Even with these high boundaries, I still felt in my heart of hearts that it was only a matter of time before I tripped again. Or got eaten by the angry lion! Given enough of the right circumstances, I would either find my way over the wall or ignore it completely and bust right through. This scared me. But not nearly enough!

You see, the irony occurring simultaneously was that I believed—I wanted to believe—that I was better. I had "eliminated the threats" and I wanted everyone to just move on—my wife especially—and be happy. This scared me even more; though I knew I was still in danger, I wanted to ignore it completely. This is the messed-up kind of thinking we have in our addictions.

The second incredible gift God gave me came two months later. By this time, the white-knuckling pattern of my life had become status quo, and sixty days of "sobriety" had me thinking maybe I had this nailed. My wife and I attended our district conference, a gathering of about one hundred churches of our denominational stripe, where Dr. Ted Roberts of Pure Desire Ministries was a guest speaker. Following his presentation, our district leadership outlined a plan where pastors could get help through Pure Desire for their struggle with pornography, not lose their jobs, and get most of it paid for. Sounds almost too good to be true, doesn't it? You would think I'd be first in line, chomping at the bit to get signed up.

You would think that. But you would also be wrong. I dragged my feet like a four-year-old on his way to bed. I wanted to believe I was okay. I wanted to quit thinking about it. But when I looked at my wife, I could still see that same look in her eyes of pain, fear, and anger all mixed together. Mostly for her benefit, I agreed to go and meet with Dr. Ted and Diane Roberts, "just to check it out." My biggest protest, honestly, was the money. The program would still cost a few grand, and I knew we just didn't have it. A convenient excuse to avoid dealing with my shame!

Before we could meet with Dr. Ted and Diane, I had to take a battery of tests online. I cruised through about a thousand questions on every kind of behavior and emotion possible. I tried my best to be honest. I felt pretty good about getting to say "no" to many of the questions. I felt pretty guilty saying "yes" to far more of them. The black-and-white objectivity of the tests started to clarify the picture of my struggle.

On the day we finally met with the Roberts, Ted pulled out my test results. There he sat, the licensed expert who had helped thousands of men navigate their way out of sexual struggles. Ted leaned across the small space that divided us, looked me in the eye, and calmly said, "Nick, you are an addict." Had he reached out and slapped me, the effect on my soul would have been no less dramatic. Though I have used that word throughout this book, that was the first moment in my life that anyone else had ever applied it to me. It was an affront. It hurt. I felt like I had been punched in the gut. But it was true.

After our appointment that day, my wife and I were driving home and she asked, "So, what did you think?" I replied, "I can't believe Ted called me an addict." The wound was still fresh and I was reeling from the impact of his words. But on that drive, the truth of the statement started to soak into the soil of my heart. Things started to make sense.

While I had never used the word about myself, as a pastor I knew quite a bit about addiction. An addiction is a behavior that has grown in our life to the point where we no longer control it, but it controls us. An addiction has been so deeply wound into our life that though we may fight against it, we are powerless to stop it. I had watched addictions ruin countless lives in my ten-plus years of ministry. What I hadn't noticed was the point at which my sexual behaviors had crossed the line from craving to an addiction.

I discovered that applying the word to my behavior actually brought a great deal of freedom. As strange as that may sound, it gave me permission to take a deep breath and finally accept the reality of my situation and the depth of the problem I had. Up until then, I had convinced everyone, including myself, that this really wasn't a problem. Owning up to the truth that I had an addiction meant accepting that I really did have a problem. When I accepted this, I could be broken in the right way. I could die to myself, which is what needed to happen all along.

GOD'S STORY: ONLY ONE CAN RAISE THE DEAD

One of my all-time favorite movie series, and books for that matter, is *The Lord of the Rings*. Early in the first movie, two wise, aged wizards are having a heated debate about the proper approach to handling a ring of great power. The one, Gandalf, sees the ring as a great evil and believes firmly that it must be destroyed. The other, Saruman, wants to use the ring to enter into a partnership with the great evil force of their day, the dark wizard Sauron. Gandalf makes a classic statement in their exchange: "There is only one lord of the ring and he does not share power."[12] The choice they faced was between submitting willingly to Sauron and his tyranny or attempting to destroy the ring and end his power. But to try and use the ring to become like Sauron would only bring them to a bitter end. The ring would only serve one master.

If we could flip this around and make it a positive statement rather than a negative, we will begin to understand something unique about God. There is only one Lord of life, and He does not share power. We can come willingly under His reign and enjoy His life, or we can fight against it. We can either be for Him or against Him, but to try to *become* Him is impossible. Here's what I mean.

On the Mount of Olives, Jesus prayed to God on the night before His death. This is quite an amazing picture: the Son of God on His knees before the Father God, on the cusp of fulfilling His God-given mission in the world. Now try and imagine that you had never read this passage before. If you have been reading the Gospels up to this point, you would know that Jesus saw Himself as the Son of God, having come from God and returning to Him. You would also know that Jesus was very clear on His purpose—that He had come to die, even knowing that His death would be harsh at the hands of the Pharisees and Jewish leaders. He is the sacrificial Lamb of God, as John the Baptist calls Him on the day of His baptism (John 1:29). From this reading, you would also know that Jesus fully expected to be raised from the dead (Luke 18:31-33). He knew ahead of time what was going to happen.

So if you knew all this and then turned the page to where Jesus prays to the Father the night before His death, how would you expect Him to pray? In my mind, I would expect Jesus to be praying for strength, preparing His mind and body for what was to come, and to be praying for the will to endure. I might also expect Him to ask that the moments pass quickly and then rejoice that He was soon to be reunited with the Father. I would expect gratefulness that the time for fulfilling His mission had come. Wouldn't you expect this as well?

But that wasn't Jesus' prayer. Not even close. Jesus prayed, "Father, if you are willing, please take this cup of suffering away from me." He was so moved by agony and pain that the Bible says His sweat fell like great drops of blood. I'm not entirely sure what that means, but I do know that it means this is serious business. This is not "now I lay me down to sleep" kind of praying. This is do-or-die kind of stuff! Now isn't that odd? Jesus had already prophesied over and over that He *would* die, that this is the reason He had come, and also that He *would* be raised to life again. Why this sudden request for it all *not* to happen?

I don't think Jesus was scared. I think Jesus knew His job. From day one of His public ministry when His cousin John baptized Him, Jesus had been identified as the Lamb of God. This imagery harkens back to the Old Testament pattern of a pure, spotless lamb being butchered each Passover to cover the sins of the people. The lamb's only job in that story was to die, a powerless character fulfilling his role in a much larger drama.

Similarly, at this moment in His life, Jesus had control over one thing only: surrendering His life to death. He said it this way: "No one can take my life from me. I sacrifice it voluntarily. For I have the authority to lay it down when I want to and also to take it again. For this is what my Father has commanded" (John 10:18). In other words, the ability to surrender Himself to death—or choose not to—was in Jesus' hands only. He controlled what He did with His life. In speaking of Himself, Jesus also said, "Very truly I tell you, unless a kernel of wheat falls to the ground and dies, it remains only a single seed. But if it dies, it produces many seeds" (John 12:24 NIV).

What all of this means is that as a fully human being, Jesus didn't control what happened after He died. He did not have the power to bring His own body back from the dead. He was fully human, and so dead would really mean dead. His entire job was to die and then entrust Himself to the One who raises the dead. Jesus could not participate in His death while also experiencing His resurrection. So, on the mountain that night, I think Jesus prayed in great agony and sweated drops of blood because He was entirely focused on His job: death. When this fills His mind, He is moved to cry out to God, "Spare me!" He wasn't looking three days around the corner to a resurrection. That was God's business and God's job. God had not asked Jesus to come and be raised from the dead; He had asked Jesus to come and be the Lamb. And the Lamb's job is a difficult and painful one. Jesus prays as He prays because His job was to die.

I think the Apostle Paul grabs hold of this idea in his writing. In the book of Philippians, Paul wrote about considering everything in his life to be rubbish—absolute garbage—in comparison to knowing Christ. He had gladly given up everything else in order to be one with Christ. "I can really know Christ and experience the mighty power that raised him from the dead. I can learn what it means to suffer with him, *sharing in his death*, so that somehow, I can experience the resurrection from the dead" (Philippians 3:10-11, my paraphrase). All of Paul's effort here is on dying. Paul wants to share in the *experience* of the resurrection of Christ and the mighty power. But in order to do so, he realizes accurately that he must *learn and share* in Christ's death. To experience something is a more passive posture; to learn and share requires an aggressive participation.

To the church in Rome, Paul also wrote, "Or have you forgotten that when we were joined with Christ Jesus in baptism, *we joined him in his death*? For we died and were buried with Christ by baptism. And just as Christ was raised from the dead by the glorious power of the Father, now we also may live new lives" (Romans 6:3-4, italics mine). Paul points out a great tendency of ours: We are prone to forget the part about dying and become overly focused on the living.

Jesus made a very bold call to those who wanted to be His disciples. He proclaimed, "If any of you want to be my follower, you must turn from your selfish ways, take up your cross, and follow me. If you try to hang on to your life, you will lose it. But if you give up your life for my sake and for the sake of the Good News, you will save it" (Mark 8:34-35). How are we to follow after Jesus, according to this Scripture? By taking up our cross. In this context, to this audience, the cross only meant one thing: death. Literal, physical, painful death. For the first-century Jew, the cross had not yet become a symbol, a gold trinket worn around the neck to symbolize our faith preference. For them, the cross meant the most brutal means by which criminals died under the Roman regime. The cross meant death—hard, bloody, agonizing death. Jesus tells all His would-be followers that their job is just like His. We must die. It is only through "giving up our life" that we can ever find it.

For the entirety of my struggle with pornography up until 2010, I had been trying to die while simultaneously planning my resurrection. I had been trying to figure out how to make things better for myself and others even as I dealt with the problem. I wanted to hold the power of death *and* life in my hands. But Jesus taught and modeled something so clear to me: My job is no less than His. Jesus became the Savior of the world because He willingly gave His body up to death. And if I want to experience His saving, freeing power in my life, then I must follow Him into death. If I want to know the resurrection, then I must put all of my effort into dying. And so also must you. The path to life is through death. Your job is to die: God's job is to raise the dead. And He does not share this power.

OUR STORY: PLANNING YOUR FUNERAL

This seems kind of odd, doesn't it? That the Breakthrough Peak I'm describing to you is all about going up the hill to die? In our world, we are taught the opposite. Life comes through effort, achievement, and hard work. We are told to pull ourselves up by our bootstraps, live the American dream, and be a man who stands bravely against the world and do whatever needs doing: tough, rugged, and usually alone. How out of tune does going up a mountain to die sound with this symphony playing behind us? And yet, how out of tune was it for Jesus to go up a mountain and die a criminal's death two thousand years ago? He was supposed to be the Messiah, the one to redeem Israel from harsh Roman rule. Instead, He hung on a cross. It was foolishness. The world laughed.

The religious mocked. Even fellow death-row hangers tossed their derisive words His direction: "If you really are God, save yourself."

But Jesus died anyway. And the world has never been the same.

In your struggle with lust and pornography, you face this same decision. Will you try to ascend the mountain of freedom through your effort, your power, and your "trying harder?" Will you grin and bear it, get 'er done, and choose your own destiny? Or…will you choose to die? Your choice is no less out of tune with the world now than Jesus' was then, but it is the decision that will change your life. As C. S. Lewis says, "Nothing that has not died will be resurrected."[13]

When you die, God can finally raise the dead. (That's you, by the way.) Have you come to the point where you are willing to die? Up until the moment you make this decision, your battle against lust and pornography will always be a repetitive cycle of victory and failure. You are working on your resurrection, your life, while also planning your death. It is not possible. Your job, like Jesus, is to die.

The Apostle Paul tells us to "put to death the sinful, earthly things lurking within you" (Colossians 3:5) and to "consider yourselves to be dead to the power of sin and alive to God through Christ Jesus" (Romans 6:11). Over and over, Scripture teaches us to die.

I know that by now you want to push back and say, "Hey, wait a minute. Scripture is filled with all kinds of verses and ideas about living the new life, following the Spirit, and being confident of our hope in Christ. Are you saying we are supposed to ignore all that?" No! Absolutely not. What I *am* saying is that we never deal with sin by self-effort. When it comes to dealing with sin and struggle in our life, our *primary* work is to die to self. In doing this, we set ourselves up in a place where our proceeding effort is not self-centered, but Christ-centered. We cannot be filled with His life unless we die to our old life.

WHAT DOES IT LOOK LIKE TO DIE?

First and foremost, this means acknowledging that you can't do this. You do not have what it takes to set yourself free and create lasting change. I reached a point where I was completely broken—in my pride, in my ego, in my belief that I could do this and figure it out, in my belief that it would just go away, and in my refusal to accept that I had a problem. I had been running away from this for so long that to finally "give up" in terms of my self-effort was incredibly freeing. I was broken and finally willing to "face the darkness"—to let go of my efforts and see what happened next. This is the first decision you must make.

Secondly, this decision to die means admitting that you truly need others—and not just for more accountability. You need someone else to tell you how to crawl out of this hole because you have tried and slipped back down so many times before. The very nature of addiction and struggle is creating protective barriers that blind and delude you to the truth of your behaviors. Because of sin, you have lost the ability to truly see yourself. So you must finally be willing to be vulnerable and real at the deepest level.

Finally, dying to self means surrender—surrendering to a process that is not your own, surrendering to others, and surrendering to God's way of redemption. You have been working your plan for long enough, and it's not working. Dying to self means dying to your way of creating change and opening your life up to new ideas, new methods, and new authority in your life. Surrender is always scary because it means loss of control. But remember: you can either fight against God or you can come under His reign. In order to come under His reign and experience the life and joy He has for you, you must put down the ring of self-effort and stop trying to be god of your own life. God's unique way of redemption is not self-help, but rejoining community with Him. And this always requires community with others. The path to community is always the same. This is the other half of the Shame Cycle, and we'll discuss it soon in chapter 8.

The question before you now is: "Are you ready to hurt enough to find true freedom?" I have to be as honest with you as I can be and say that death—dying to self—is hard work. The journey is far more painful than I ever expected, but also far more liberating. It is the kind of pain that changes us and leaves us better, not bitter. The path will actually get harder before it gets easier because once you surrender, you will finally begin facing the places in your heart and mind where you have erected a barrier of lust and sexuality around them in order to feel good. When you die to self and stop all the self-protecting schemes, pain is the inevitable consequence. But unmasking this pain and dealing with core issues is where everything begins.

Here's a great truth: When I began this process with Pure Desire, I believed that my life was essentially good, except for this *problem* I had with pornography. I thought that if I could just deal with the problem, everything else was okay. What I discovered, however, is that pornography was only a *symptom* of much deeper issues in my heart and soul. Pornography was the overflow and the outlet for my areas of people-pleasing, performing for approval, and trying to measure up to other men. Pornography became the lens into my soul by which I was able to truly see myself for the first time.

And this is the most amazing part: When I began to tackle pornography head on, *all* the issues began to change. I had spent five years and $25,000 going to a seminary so I could grow as a leader. One year of addressing my struggle with pornography changed me more than the five years of higher education ever did. When I died to self and began facing gut-level truth about myself, everything else began to change. And the same will happen for you, if you make the choice to die.

In the book, *A Grace Disguised*, author Gerald Sittser recounts having a recurring nightmare after a tragic car accident claimed the lives of his wife, his mother, and his daughter. Harry Flanagan references this story in a portion he wrote for the *Seven Pillars of Freedom* workbook. He says it well, so I will quote him and Sittser for a bit:

> In the nightmare, Sittser would be on an endless beach with the sun low in the early evening sky. Darkness seemed to be gathering in the eastern sky and he feared being swallowed up in the darkness. Sittser would begin to run as hard as he could toward the setting sun hoping that he would be able to stay in the daylight. His nightmare ended in stark terror just as the sun set below the horizon and he was immersed in the darkness. Sittser would be exhausted and drenched in perspiration after thrashing in bed as he ran toward the setting sun.
>
> Sittser had this horrible dream every night for several weeks. This nightmare was consuming him in every way whether he was awake or asleep. Sittser finally called his sister and told her of the dream. She responded with an incredible and insightful comment. She told her brother that nobody could catch the setting sun; she told him to **turn, face the darkness, even run into the darkness, for in so doing he would catch the rising sun.**[14]

How long have you run from the pain and consequences of your struggle? How much have you endured in trying to "catch the setting sun?" Friend, it is time to stop running, let your arms fall to your sides, and turn into the darkness. Let all that you fear come right at you. This is dying to self at its best! For in so doing, the Morning Star (Revelation 22:16) will rise in your life and bring you light and life that you have *never* experienced before. Choosing to die is a challenge, yes, but it is the only way to experience the resurrection light of Christ.

DO I HAVE TO HIT ROCK BOTTOM FIRST?

By now you might be wondering this very thing. Is experiencing tremendous, life-changing pain the only way to Breakthrough Peak? Do we have to crash in a bloody heap at the bottom before we start climbing out? For many of us, this is what it takes. In fact, you may be reading this book because you're there already. You wife said, "Deal with this or I'm gone." You're on the verge of losing a relationship, a family, or a job. Or maybe you've lost them already. This pain is not fun and I would not wish it on anyone, but I hope you're seeing by now that this pain will transform you for the better. If you will let it.

My answer to your question, "Do I have to hit rock bottom first?" would be: not necessarily. Hitting rock bottom is what it takes for most of us to be broken in the right places. Only the shattering of this impact jars us loose from self-sufficiency and "trying harder." *The secret, though, is not in hitting rock bottom; the secret is in surrender.* We must come to a place where we will accept that we can't do this in our own power. It will take every ounce of strength we have, but that doesn't mean we have the strength to do this. This brings us to a place of surrender and death.

Now hear this: I believe with all my heart that you can *choose* this place; you can choose to take the power to change out of your own hands and put it into the hands of God and others. Anthony de Mello, in his book, *Awareness*, reminds us that most people aren't really looking to change. "Most people tell you they want to get out of kindergarten, but don't believe them. Don't believe them! All they want you to do is to mend their broken toys. 'Give me back my wife. Give me back my job. Give me back my money. Give me back my reputation, my success.' This is what they want, they want their toys replaced. What they want is relief; a cure is painful."[15]

If you have a strong desire to change, to really change and not just relieve the pain, you can experience Breakthrough. It's okay and normal to want the stuff back and to want to relieve the pain, but if that's all you're after, true change will not occur. If you're willing to face the pain of a process, a journey toward freedom, then a cure—a real and lasting cure—is possible! How do I know? Because I know the God who raises the dead and I am experiencing His resurrection power in my life. I'm watching it unfold in others. So get on the path. The path to freedom is about to begin.

THE LINCHPIN: I WOULD DO ANYTHING

One of the frequent lines I used with my wife when I would confess my addiction (again) was, "I will do anything you want me to. Just name it, and I will do that." I wanted desperately to make her happy. I wanted her to not be angry and to not leave. It is sadly ironic to me that, at the time, I was more willing to pacify her emotions than to actually change my heart and my behaviors. When we reached our breaking point, God brought this line back to me. I was balking at the process with Pure Desire;

I was giving excuses about the time and the money; and I was dragging my feet about jumping in. God whispered to me at that time, "You have told your wife over and over that you would do anything for her. Now's the time to prove it!"

I'm not so sure I liked that challenge, but God was right on. Big surprise, right? Up until that moment, I had been all talk and just enough action to delude my wife, others, and myself into thinking that progress was occurring. Now was the time to be all action and no talk. (Or at least a lot less!)

This is the time for fewer promises and more commitments. Guarantee less, but actually *do* more. When we come to the place of being willing to do anything rather than stay where we are, God can move in and bring true, lasting change. This place is a raw combination of pain, truth, and desperation discovered when we reach the end of self-sufficiency.

This is also the place God has been waiting for us to reach. On the hike I described at the beginning of this chapter, I experienced something incredible. After what seemed like hours (in truth, probably more like fifteen minutes) of scaling the mountain in adverse weather conditions, we emerged alive and intact on the summit. And at that moment, a wonderful and surprising thing happened. The storm broke, the clouds dispersed, and Sunlight Peak lived up to her name. In striking beauty, rays of warm, stunning sunshine began to light up the entire topography around us. It was truly awe-inspiring. We stood there as a group and sang the old hymn, "How Great Thou Art." I felt in my heart that creation sang with us that day.

As I looked back down the way we had come, I was surprised to see how innocent and plain our trail now seemed. In the clouds and the storm, the terrain we had crossed felt treacherous and deadly. In the light and calm of a fresh afternoon, the path looked wide, the slope gentle, and the way clear. After we had lingered for some time enjoying the vista, we descended down this route with ease, joy, and satisfaction.

Friends, we have been scrambling over the rocky path of self-deception and failed self-effort. But at the end of our path, when we die to self, the brilliant sun of God's light will shine upon us. He invites us on to Breakthrough Peak, to come up the mountain with Christ and die to self so He can raise us anew in Christ Jesus. If you will let this happen, you will one day look back down the path and wonder why it seemed so hard. The light will break on you and things will become clear.

You die. He will make you a new creation.

> *"Awake, O sleeper, rise up from the dead,*
> *and Christ will give you light!"* Ephesians 5:14b

AND FINALLY...

I wrote this poem for my wife early in our journey toward freedom. I think it depicts the brutal truth for all of us who have tried to pacify this beast in our lives only to realize the beast had come to take over and pacification was not an option. I'm no poet, but I pray this gives you a greater vision of what must happen in your life:

MY BEAUTY AND MY BEAST
(Nick J. Stumbo, February 17, 2010)

One day my beauty and I went out
  And spread a blanket beneath the trees.
Our minds were set upon one task
  To spend the day in love's blissful ease.

My beauty laid her head upon my arm
  And rested in peaceful security there.
I gazed deeply into her loving eyes
  As I gently stroked her golden hair.

But our idyllic scene was broken by
  The sudden shaking of a bush so near.
Bursting out from behind this leaf
  Came a beast to inspire great fear.

My beauty cowered in my shadow,
  Fearing the worst to come.
But in bravado I comforted her,
  "Don't worry, I know this one."

For indeed, this lustful animal was mine,
  Who tracked with me day and night.
"I can handle him, so be at peace;
  There's no reason for such fright."

So over I went to reason
  With our uninvited guest.
I conjured and cajoled with him
  Till he went away to rest.

I returned to my beauty's side
  There in our peaceful glade,
Unaware that on her chest
  A deep cut my beast had made.

For time on end, this scene
  Predictably played over and over,
Each time inflicting a deeper wound
  Near the heart of my true lover.

But blind I was to the pain it caused
    Until at last she began to weep.
"I'm perishing," she cried,
    "At the cruel hands of your beast."

And there she wilted in my arms,
    Alas her strength was spent.
I cried out in anguish to the heavens,
    My own heart was finally rent.

And then the gracious One,
    Who is wise beyond all measure,
Came unseen and laid a sword
    Silently there upon the heather.

I grasped it firm and strode
    To where my beast must again appear.
And when he did I boldly cried,
    "Beast your end is near!"

How cunningly he softly sang
    That it didn't have to be this way.
Just let him be, he begged of me
    And promised to stay at bay.

But with one more glance at the wounds of my beauty
    I knew that I could delay no more.
I plunged the sword deep into the heart of my beast
    And pierced him to the core.

In agony and screams of death,
    My beast crumpled at my feet
As at that moment a voice began to sing
    Gently, softly, perfectly and sweet.

It was freedom's song finally loosed
      From chains within my heart.
I lifted up my voice in chorus,
      Singing, "My God, how great thou art."

And back I turned to my beauty there,
      Still lying at death's door.
I held her tight and looked to Heaven,
      Pleading for mercy once more.

Then in astonishment I watched the wounds
      That had covered her gracious form
Begin to fade and disappear,
      And her skin began to warm.

Her eyes she opened in newfound love,
      Gazing up at me.
"Is he gone?" she asked.
      "Can we finally be free?"

"Forever, my beauty," I said to her,
      "The battle at last is won.
You and I shall ever be
      Joyful dancers beneath a clear sun."

One day my beauty and I went out
      And spread a blanket beneath the trees.
And at last we knew that we were free
      To spend the day in love's blissful ease.

PART 3: THE HEALING PATH

CHAPTER SEVEN | THE JOY OF INTIMACY

"You ain't seen nothing yet. B-b-b-baby, you ain't seen nothing yet!" Or so say the lyrics of the classic 1970's tune. Though this song was written before I was born, I was about to experience the truth of these words in a very real way. My wife and I met with Dr. Ted and Diane Roberts in June 2010. Due to a mission trip to Eastern Europe, our family summer vacation, and my own hesitations, we didn't start our recovery program in earnest until August of that year. But when we started, it was total immersion! As Ted likes to say, "You have to make this a top-shelf priority. Nothing else matters right now except for this." I found out he was serious. Our decision to go on the Pure Desire journey was a decision for me to face this issue, and the truth about the pain it was causing, head on.

I walked out of their office with an armload of books. I began working my way through three separate workbooks; my wife had two of her own. I was doing monthly ninety-minute Skype counseling sessions with Harry Flanagan; my wife and I did monthly ninety-minute marriage counseling sessions; and every three months we would spend a full day in Gresham with Dr. Ted and Diane, just the four of us. These days were intense, draining, and incredibly powerful.

In addition to this counseling load, my wife and I were both meeting regularly with recovery groups at a larger church 30 minutes north of us—me in a group of addicts, and her in a group of wives hurt by their husbands' addictions. At times, it felt like we ate, drank, and slept with Pure Desire on the brain. I thought I had been "serious" about making change earlier in my life. Those past efforts now felt like fighting a forest fire with a squirt gun, which is pretty accurate in terms of the effectiveness those efforts had on my behaviors. We were now fighting this fire with twenty-ton barrels of flame-retardant, an all-out aerial assault. And change was actually happening. Not just behavior modification, but a renewing of the heart and mind.

To top it all off, I got to take a polygraph. This may have been the most painful moment of my life. If you have never had the "opportunity" to experience a polygraph, let me give you a brief summary. You walk into a place you have likely never been and sit across the table from a man you have never seen. He proceeds to ask you two hours worth of the most invasive, personal questions you can imagine about everything you have ever done. The only acceptable responses are "yes" or "no." No gray areas. No "maybe, but let me explain that one." After this two-hour grilling where you feel about as low about yourself as possible, you get hooked up to the machine. It all feels very Hollywood-like. Based on all of the information you have provided during the two-hour grilling, you answer ten questions about whether or not you have been honest and about any topics of specific interest to the person requiring the polygraph (in my case, Pure Desire). Pass means that you have told the truth and have no more hidden skeletons or locked closets. Fail means that you are hiding, lying, deceiving, or a concoction of all three. This test is like a sledgehammer to all of your denial schemes.

I passed. And I felt terrible. Imagine taking every sin, great and small, you have ever committed or thought to commit and laying them all out on the table with a total stranger. This was a humbling place to be! As my wife and I drove home from this experience, I recounted to her how dirty it made me feel to see all my sin at one time. Then I found myself getting emotional, an experience that was becoming fairly common by that time in the process. Maybe I was just spent from the emotional toll of the interview, but I think it was something more. As I thought about the interview on that drive home, I felt as though God were saying, again, "Look at it. That's how sinful you are. Now do you understand the depth of My love and forgiveness? That is the Nick Stumbo I have forgiven with the blood of My Son, Jesus Christ." Never had I seen myself more clearly as a sinner. And never had I understood grace more clearly.

In short, what all of the counseling, workbooks, group meetings, and testing meant is that my wife and I began to really talk. A lot. More than I had ever talked before. My wife loved it and even said she felt like we were dating again. Evidently, when I was first intent on wooing and winning my wife's heart, I was quite the conversationalist. Over the last ten years of marriage, I had slipped more into an "I talked all day at work, let's just watch a movie" mode. For her to say it felt like we were dating again was a bit of an odd statement, though, because we had some very painful talks over the next twelve months as I became honest about my fears, the subtle darkness behind many of my behaviors and patterns, and all the ways I had hidden myself from her and from others.

Maybe you've been taught an idea like this: "Men don't have emotions." Ha! Don't believe that garbage for a moment. We have them—maybe even more than our wives—but we don't know how to express them. We grow up learning to stuff them, hide them, or express them through anger, aggression, or showmanship. In this season of honestly opening up to my wife, I discovered that I did have emotions and I began to process what was going on in my head. I found that I had some very painful opinions about myself that were driving my behaviors. To face them was difficult, but it also brought freedom.

We cried, we talked, and on some nights, we just sat looking at each other. We stayed up many nights way past when reasonable adults were supposed to go to bed. And somehow, it was all very energizing. We were actually talking about real stuff, not just the kids and the weather and our schedule, but our hopes, our dreams, and our fears. Though these conversations were often intense and at times painful, we grew closer than we had ever been as a married couple because my wife really knew me. And she accepted me still, which took the change to a whole new level.

An unexpected side effect was how much this year of confession, honesty, and conversation touched on our sex life: It got better. A lot better. We had actually been doing pretty well before; my wife somewhat believed she could fix me by being sexually responsive to my needs. While this was very much appreciated on my part in those days, it did little to change me, as I alluded to previously. Now, however, our life of intimacy became rich, deep, and fulfilling. Not with new methods, positions, or tricks, but with a deeper trust and connection already in place. Rather than having sex to feel close, we enjoyed one another because we were close. Sex wasn't merely about feeling good, but about the expression of the connection we had and the love we shared.

This also did something very good within my brain. Suddenly, the addictive nature of sex was working completely in my favor. Remember, God designed sex as a kind of relational glue that would hold married couples together. When God did this, He brilliantly designed our minds in such a way that sex shared exclusively with a spouse would actually create a heightened desire for more of the same. Mark Driscoll writes about how the chemicals released in our brain when we have sex are so powerful that they essentially bind a man to whatever caused it. "The natural chemical 'high', what some call a 'biochemical love potion', resulting from sex and orgasm was designed by God to bind a husband and wife together. In the best sense of the word, God intends for a devoted married couple to be 'addicted' to each other, bound together in every way."[16] This aspect of God's creation began to work for us in amazing ways.

When we think of our sexuality, culture has taught us that what we need is a buffet: We have different tastes and desires, so we need a spread of different choices and options. To just eat the same thing over and over would be routine, dull, and lifeless. So, we keep filling our plate at the lust buffet with different images, different women, and different routines. Yet, in the end, we are left feeling the same: unfulfilled, unsatisfied, and let down. What God teaches—and research on the brain bears this out to be true—is that when we focus on one dish, our brain is designed to increase the hunger for that dish. The cultural way of sex creates a greater appetite with less satisfaction, while God's road focuses our desire while delivering a far greater payoff. If that doesn't make you pause for a moment and appreciate the beauty of God's design, I don't know what will! (For a thorough treatment of this idea, I highly encourage you to pick up a copy of *Wired for Intimacy* by William Struthers.) I would be prone to doubt that these statements are true, expect for the fact that my wife began to experience these truths in profound ways. Not perfectly, for sure, but like God at creation, we found ourselves regularly stepping back to say, "It was good."

MY WIFE'S FAVORITE DAY

My wife will tell you that one of the greatest days of her life was when I told our church I had an addiction to pornography. You may find that hard to believe, so let me explain. After working the Pure Desire track for more than nine months, Dr. Ted Roberts determined that we were far enough along that we should share our journey with the church. From day one, I had known that public disclosure would be part of this process, but I had successfully put the thought out of my mind for quite awhile. So when Ted said we were ready, I took a deep breath and began working through what to say. The emphasis of sharing was not to be a "woe is me, I'm such a sinner" confessional, but an honest assessment of where I had been and what God had done in setting me free.

On March 27, 2011, in a sermon entitled, "Getting Unstuck," I shared the following statement with our church body. This is a bit of a diversion from the flow of the book, but I think it might be helpful for you to see how this topic was handled in a church crowd that rarely, if ever, broached the subject of human sexuality:

Let me take a minute and tell you why this topic is so important to me and why I have the ability to bring some unique perspective. Today, I am not simply talking about addictions through the lens of others and their experience. I am not merely telling you about the hope and healing that others have discovered. Today, I have been sharing through the lens of my own addiction and in the joy of hope and healing that I have found.

Yes, I did say my own addiction. For some of you, it may be incredibly disconcerting to hear your pastor use that word about himself. For others, it may be incredibly freeing to hear that your pastor is a normal human being. But no matter your reaction, the truth remains. I was an addict. In my late teens, I began regularly viewing pornographic magazines. In college, access to the Internet took this obsession to a whole new level. I loved Jesus and was even preparing to serve Him in full-time ministry, and yet this battle raged on in my soul. The emotion finally bubbled over during those college years into confession to a good friend who became my accountability partner. "Finally," I thought, "now that it's in the open I will be free of it."

But the opposite actually proved to be true. Without sufficient resources to truly change in a deep way, the behavior continued with more shame and guilt than ever before. So began a painful cycle of acting out, hiding behavior, and living in shame, until I could bear it no more and confession would occur. This binge-purge cycle of sin continued into my marriage and into ministry. Mistakes would be made, and so more promises and commitments would be given to those who loved me and trusted me. And though some growth occurred and periods of abstinence were observed, the addiction continued.

In this system of sin-management, I convinced myself that I was doing okay. Sure, it cropped up from time to time, but surely I wasn't as bad as others and I thought that if I just kept believing and praying, sooner or later it would go away. Well, it didn't. Fourteen months ago, I was still stuck. But at this time, God gave me a tremendous gift—the gift of pain. He opened my eyes to see how my behaviors, which I thought were minor, were subtly, yet steadily, destroying my wife, my ministry, and even my faith.

For the first time in my life I realized that sin-management was not enough. Real change—deep change—had to occur, but I didn't know *where to begin. At the time, God brought another precious gift to my wife and me through our district office. At our annual conference, they announced a partnership with Dr. Ted Roberts and his ministry, Pure Desire near Portland. In May of last year, we begin an intense and intentional process with Ted and his wife, Diane, pastors themselves and also experts on addiction and recovery. We sat with counselors who loved Jesus, understood the human heart and the human brain, and who knew a path to freedom. We began attending a weekly support and recovery group in Chehalis, me for sexual addicts and my wife for those who had been hurt by them. For the first time, I was able to process my life's journey and find that pornography was not the real problem to be dealt with, but it was a symptom of much deeper issues in my life. Because of deep needs I had for finding my value through performance and my identity through success, I became hooked on the false promises of pornography as a way to medicate my pain and disappointment. Making this connection took me from behavior management to deep heart change.*

For the first time in my life, I was able to face the lies of Satan that were operating in the background of my life. Because of this addiction, I had believed myself to be a bad person, someone whom God tolerated because of how hard I worked for Him. Through the patient love and grace of Dr. Ted and Diane Roberts and others, I have discovered the awesome and life-changing reality of God's love. What were once just words have now truly become the cornerstone of my life.

While I must forever be on my guard against sliding back in this direction, I do want you to know that without a doubt I am healthier than I have ever been. Our marriage is stronger than it has ever been. And I am a better pastor than I have ever been, not because of growth in skill, but because of change of heart. I no longer have to serve God to find His approval and love; I am finally free to serve Him, and you, because He already loves and approves of me.

So, I stand before you today as a recovering addict. I know that as your pastor, you have called me and anointed me and asked me to lead you well, but in this area of my life I have failed at that. I am a human being who has struggled, and I am sorry that I allowed this addiction to overcome me. I seek your forgiveness for that. And I invite you and give you the freedom to approach me—to process this with me. I know that some of you don't want that, won't need that, and that's okay; but as others of you do process this, don't hesitate to talk to me.

I realize that some of you don't know me well, or you might be visiting here this weekend, and you probably weren't expecting this level of honesty. But I hope you do see in this the real power of the gospel—that Jesus loves us not because we are religious or holy, but He loves us in our humanity and in our weakness—and we want East Hills to be the kind of place where that can be lived out and experienced by everyone, including the pastor.

What I am confident of, as Paul tells us in Romans 8, is that God is at work in this situation for His good and for His glory. What has happened in my life and in our marriage is not for me alone, but it is also for you. The freedom I have found is no credit to me; it is because someone who knew the way showed it to me and walked the path with me in order to help me truly find Christ. And now I want to do the same for you. God is at work in this, and He is at work in our church to bring freedom to you, and to men all over Cowlitz County.

For ten years of ministry, my secret addiction had been my wife's greatest burden. Only for her, it had a wicked twist. Since it was my secret, I could make the choice to share it with trusted friends or colleagues when I felt safe enough to do so. But for her, she did not have this liberty. She felt she couldn't talk to anyone because it wasn't her secret to tell. Pure Desire had finally given her an outlet and a place to talk. This was a big step. But when I confessed openly, she no longer had to hide. She was finally free. The results were overwhelming. She received numerous cards and emails of support and encouragement. And unbidden, she had half a dozen gals come up to her and ask if she would start a group for women, just like the one she had been attending up north. In a single day, a ministry to men *and their wives* was launched.

For me, the public disclosure drove home the point I had been learning through times of honest conversation with my wife: When we are real about our issues, people who love us do not run away. They run toward us with the grace and mercy of God. On that weekend, I was loved, hugged, and affirmed like never before. This, I believe, is part of the mystery of Christ in us: We can't help but move toward the repentant heart. Countless people told me it was my best message ever; the day I confessed what a bugger I had been was their favorite message of all! That day, my wife and I both learned through others a central truth about God: He runs toward the broken.

GOD'S STORY: WE ARE THE PROSTITUTE (GULP)

One of my favorite stories in Scripture has to be the lived-out parable of Hosea and Gomer. Hosea was an Old Testament prophet at the time of the divided kingdom, Israel in the north and Judea in the south. Both kingdoms were in the midst of an on-again, off-again relationship with God. The people would serve Him for a time, and then be seduced by the false gods and false promises of foreign nations. They continued to provoke God to righteous anger by their adulterous hearts.

At the beginning of Hosea and Gomer's story, God came along with a message for Hosea: "When the LORD first began speaking to Israel through Hosea, he said to him, 'Go and marry a prostitute so some of her children will be conceived in prostitution'" (Hosea 1:2). This was Hosea's call to ministry! Go and marry an unfaithful woman who will continue to be unfaithful to you. How many of us would have accepted that offer? But God wanted to give the people a practical demonstration of the depths of His love for them.

Hosea obeyed God and married the prostitute named Gomer. In their marriage, they had three children, though from the introduction above, it is highly likely that these children were not all fathered by Hosea. And as sad as that is, it may have been the high point of their marriage, because the next thing Gomer did was leave. After being redeemed by Hosea and given status in his home (very important in that pre-modern world), she walked right out the door and back to the life she knew. She sold her body and her soul to other men and defiled all that is sacred.

For a Jewish man of that day and age, this would have made Gomer reprehensible and unclean, impossible to ever love again. This makes God's next command to Hosea so shockingly absurd, "Then the LORD said to me [Hosea], 'Go and love your wife again. Bring her back to you and love her, even though she loves adultery'" (Hosea 3:1, my paraphrase). She loved adultery, but she didn't love Hosea or God. She loved her sin. Even so, Hosea is called to go and get her again because "the Lord still loves Israel even though the people have turned to other gods, and love to worship them" (Hosea 3:1). God called Hosea to love her and redeem her in spite of her failures. She had been off giving away the best of herself, her "choice gifts" to undeserving suitors, but God is relentless in His love and would not let her go.

The scene is really quite poignant. We can't be sure why, but the place Hosea had to go to find his bride was the slave market. So destitute and impoverished was Gomer that she was being sold to the highest bidder, to any bidder. As she stood there ashamed and alone, the slave-master called for bids. Gomer had been around the block so many times that no one even made an offer, until a hand went up and a voice called out from the back of the room. All heads turn to see Hosea, the oft-jilted lover striding to the front of the room. "I will take her," he declared. Hosea wrapped her gently in his own robe and walked her back to his home one more time. Though Gomer deserved nothing, Hosea gave her back all things: a home, a place, and her dignity.

Now here is the catch. We usually think we're supposed to be Hosea—love the unlovable, go after the forgotten, and forgive even when it hurts. We also think we are supposed to learn about God—our Heavenly Father loves, heals, and forgives all sin. But I wonder if we have ever gone far enough to really and truly identify ourselves with Gomer. We are the prostitute. We have taken the choicest of gifts that God Himself has given us, and we've offered them to other gods. We have given away the beauty of sex for cheap thrills. We have trampled on the sacred vows of marriage for our own personal pleasure. We have misused and misspent the best of our time and income on worshipping the pornographic gods of our culture. Even though God has brought us into His home, we have walked right back out the door. But hear this: God is just as relentless in His love for you as He ever was for Gomer.

If we have ever been stuck in addiction or repetitive sin of any kind, we need to see that we are Gomer—naked, ashamed, rejected, and selling out to whoever will pay—when God comes along and pays an inordinate price for our release. God treats us not as slaves, but as sons. He wraps us in the cloak of His own mercy and grace and redeems us once more. And the Bible even tells us that to do so gives God great pleasure (Ephesians 1:5).

God told Hosea about a day that was coming for Israel, but also for us: "They will come trembling in awe to the Lord, and they will receive his good gifts in the last days" (Hosea 3:5, my paraphrase). If we have faced the depth of our sin, then we have come trembling to God in awe. How could He forgive so much? But He does. And now God is promising to give good gifts to us again. Though we have taken His choice gifts and thrown them like pearls to swine, He longs to bless us again with the riches of a relationship with Him. Even though we have run from Him. Even though, like Gomer, we have loved our idols more than God. Even though we have gone down this path a thousand times after swearing we would never do it again. God finds us and loves us. And in spite of all that we have done, He still has good plans for our lives! How amazing is that?

The truth is that because God does this for us, others will do this as well, because this is what God's love does in us. When we face the pain of our actions and choose to be honest, others who love us have the opportunity to respond with forgiveness and grace. (And even if they don't, even if the relationship is too far gone with your spouse or someone near to you because of the history of your actions, others will. Others in Christ will model His grace to you.) When we experience this kind of love in our places of greatest weakness and shame, we learn to be real. We choose humility and grow into true communion with God and others.

OUR STORY: THE INTIMACY CYCLE

Up to this point, we have ascended the Addictive Path together, analyzing and understanding many of the root issues of our addiction. We have emerged onto Breakthrough Peak, recognizing how pain becomes the catalyst for facing truth about ourselves. And now, we are on the Healing Path, where we will look at several key factors that contribute to our freedom. Jesus sets us free through a number of unexpected decisions. The next three chapters will deal with the decision to be in true community (Chapter 8), the decision to ground our identity in Christ (Chapter 9), and the decision to fully trust God and others (Chapter 10). For now, we will turn to the significance of our decision to be brutally honest, no matter the cost.

Maybe when you were a child your parents, like mine, taught you, "If you don't have anything nice to say, don't say anything at all." This thought pattern dominates our thinking in adulthood, particularly when it comes to self-disclosing un-nice and un-cute things about what we have done. We give in to the lie that everyone is better off if we just stay quiet. This lie is straight from the enemy of our souls, who wants to destroy us. Here is why we must face that lie: Facing the pain of being honest breaks the cycle of shame in our lives.

In Chapter 5, we looked at a typical pattern in our addiction called the **Shame Cycle**. Remember this? When we **sin**, we feel a level of **guilt or shame**. Guilt is the feeling that I *have done* bad. Shame takes it a step further and causes us to believe that we *are* bad. If we choose to avoid the pain of dealing with this, the only other route is **secrecy**, which leads us into **isolation** and always creates **separation** between God and us, and others. Since we are separated and filled with shame, sin is more likely to continue and the cycle pulls us down deeper and deeper. You have experienced in real terms the truth of this cycle. Now is the time to flip the pattern and discover God's design for dealing with our sin.

When you sin and face the resulting guilt or shame, you face a choice. You can either face **pain** or avoid pain. To tell the truth and be brutally honest about whatever you have said or done will be a painful admission of your weaknesses and shortcomings. In the past, you have avoided this pain. How could you not? Our culture preaches a pain-free message; life should be free of pain, and anything that causes pain should be avoided. There is a drug, a gadget, or a loan to help you avoid just about any kind of pain. So when you faced the pain of honesty, your natural, old-self inclination was to run and hide. Don't beat yourself up over this; remember that your first relatives Adam and Eve did exactly the same thing!

That was the past. Now, however, you can choose to face the pain. You can walk into the darkness, believing that this is the only way to catch the rising sun. You can embrace God's truth that this kind of pain will always be for our good; transformation will occur in us through this pain that couldn't come any other way.

Facing the pain means choosing to be **honest**. As we have discussed previously, there is a time and a place for honesty to occur. But it must occur. Through honesty, you break out of church nice. Through honesty, you let God and others in. Honesty is active rebellion against the unholy desire to look good before God and others. You aren't fooling God, and most likely you aren't fooling others as well as you think, so go for it; rebel against looking good so God can transform you on the inside.

Having chosen to be honest, you give God and others the opportunity and ability to offer **forgiveness**. Forgiveness says,

"I don't hold this against you any longer." God has eternally provided the means of forgiveness through Jesus Christ, but perhaps you have not fully experienced it. You said "the prayer" so you would go to Heaven, but you cannot get past the nagging fear that God holds a great deal against you. Choosing brutal honesty ushers you into a place of experiencing the wonder of God's complete forgiveness.

When you know that you are forgiven and God is holding nothing against you, you begin to experience true **intimacy**. This intimacy is not the result of earning or proving you are worthy of it. This intimacy is the result of being fully known and knowing fully that you are accepted in that place. When you experience this, you begin to breathe deeper. Your shoulders let down and you can relax in the presence of God and others. There is no more show to be put on, no more images to maintain, no appearances to keep up—only the freedom of being known and accepted in the truth of who you are.

Experiencing this kind of intimacy leads to **communion with God and others**. Whether you know it or not, this is what you are most looking for in life. Communion with God and others is a holy place without being religious. Communion is being with God and others in a way that affirms who you are and places the friendship that you share above any personal needs. This communion is a joyful place of peace in the presence of others who smile at the thought of you.

The **Intimacy Cycle**, like the Shame Cycle, is indeed a cycle. When you walk this path, you are spiraled upward into greater levels of intimacy and communion with God and others. As you practice honesty and forgiveness, you experience the kind of relationships that God intended for you from day one. You

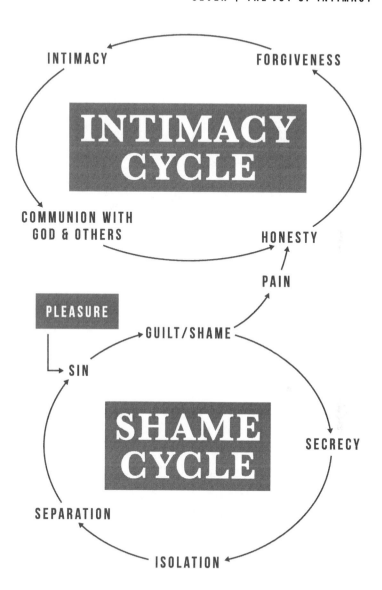

encounter a bit of "New Eden" or Heaven on earth—what the Jews call the shalom of God. What this means is that you are less likely to sin! Having broken from the Shame Cycle, you are put in right relationship with God and others, which properly fills up the places of need in your life. You don't need to run after your addictions any longer because the feelings you sought in that place are now supplied by the Giver of Life Himself. This is freedom!

You might be struggling with something here. What if you are honest and they—a spouse, a friend, a small group—don't or won't forgive? That's a fair question! First, keep in mind that forgiveness and healing may take time. When you get honest, you may be putting topics on the table that you have dealt with for years, but are very new to the person you are telling. They may need some time. You do your part by being honest and trust God do His part by bringing that person or group into forgiveness.

Second, recognize that forgiveness is ultimately from God and not any one person. After David sinned with Bathsheba, he declared, "I have sinned against the LORD" (2 Samuel 12:13). Though others may have been dramatically affected by your behavior, this is ultimately an issue between you and the Lord, and the intimacy cycle is first and foremost about our relationship with God. He's the one you have been avoiding, but now you can at last be His friend. So even if that one person withholds forgiveness, you can still experience the life-giving benefits of the Intimacy Cycle with God.

Third, when you experience forgiveness through others, this will transform you and keep you in the intimacy cycle, thus creating the greatest possibility that the one person will eventually forgive you. In other words, no one person can keep you from discovering the joy of intimacy with God. Discover true relationship with Him, and all your other relationships will eventually be affected as well.

THE BEST SEX OF YOUR LIFE

I can hear what you're thinking. *Okay, Nick, all of that relational stuff really sounds great. I know that being close to God and others is important. But in the real world I live in, I don't spend much time thinking about relationships—I just have them. How does the pain of honesty make my week better? This sounds like hard work!*

I agree. What you need to see, though, it that sexuality is a process of bonding that, up until now, you may have limited to something only physical. You have believed, perhaps, that if you could just stay physically attractive to your spouse, and she to you, that your sex life would continue to grow. But I'm guessing that you have found this simply isn't true, which should be an indicator that sex is far more than bodies. If you want great sex, work on great intimacy.

But while you work on intimacy, it would also be helpful to address some of the lies of our culture. One deceptive thought that men in general, even (or especially?) Christian men, buy into is that there is a standard of beauty. We compare women, and ourselves, to this standard in order to make decisions about our sexiness. This is crazy. The world cannot give us this standard. Driscoll says it well:

> Your standard of beauty is your spouse. One of our culture's powerful lies—fueled by pornography, sinful lust, and marketing—is that having a standard of beauty is in any way holy or helpful. God does not give us a standard of beauty—God gives us spouses. Unlike other standards of beauty, a spouse changes over time. If your spouse is skinny, you are into skinny. If your spouse is twenty, you are into twenty. When your spouse is sixty, you are no longer into twenty, but rather into sixty. And if your spouse used to be skinny, you were into skinny, but now you are into formerly skinny![17]

Is this the way you think, men? Or are your thoughts fueled by the thinking of the world? Recently, I was driving to work when the local sports radio station announced its next contest. They were calling it, "The Bigger Dance." This was shortly after the NCAA basketball tournament, March Madness, or "The Big Dance" as it is often called. This station's tournament, brackets and all, would supposedly be bigger still. As a sports enthusiast, my ears perked up at what could be so exciting.

They went on to announce that this "Bigger Dance" would be bracket of sixty-four of the most beautiful, sexy women in America. I'm not trying to sound prudish here, but I do want to point out that conversations once held only in hushed tones or in locker rooms have become common topics on public airwaves. Mentally undressing a woman is no longer hidden; it is now encouraged. We have made lusting a pastime. And then we wonder why men can't stay married. In order to find sexual fulfillment, we must reject this worldly view of beauty and embrace God's design and gift that includes one man and one woman in a marriage relationship.

Secondly, we must realize that when it comes to sex, our society has sold us a cheap imitation of God's real gift. And I'm not just talking about pornography. I am speaking of our culture's entire *idea* of sex. How do we view sex in our modern society? We see it as a means for pleasure, primarily for ourselves. So much so that masturbation, for boys or girls, is often taught as the normative experience for adolescence. Through this "innocent" behavior, the brain is trained from early on that the purpose of sex is self-pleasure. It's all about me feeling good!

Even Christian authors have been jumping on board to talk about the pleasure of sex that God created. I certainly agree with this—God intended sex for our pleasure—but we must be very clear about how this pleasure comes.

You see, everything around us in culture teaches us that pleasure comes when we get what we want. Even in a "Christian nice" way, we learn to treat our spouses kindly, be interested in meeting their needs, and take out the trash so that we can be "rewarded" later. Okay, maybe people don't or won't say it that way, but I know they think that way. I did. Sometimes I still do. The thought pattern says, "I do for you so you will do for me." This is what we are taught. But this is not God's way.

"For you have been called to live in freedom....But don't use your freedom to satisfy your sinful nature. Instead, use your freedom to serve one another in love" (Galatians 5:13). We readily apply this verse to the way we raise our children, treat our neighbors, and serve in churches. We serve one another in love. But what if we were to apply this to sex, too? What if, in our sexual intimacy with our spouse, we got serious about using our freedom to serve our spouse in love? What if we devoted our whole self to doing what pleased them?

I know. Sounds risky. We could be taken advantage of. Not appreciated. We could fail to get what we want, need, or deserve. But this is the New Testament risk that God has always taken with us: "I will give you everything and gamble that, rather than ignoring Me, it will make you turn and move toward Me." This is God's way, and healthy intimacy starts when we take God at His word and risk that serving others is actually the best way to meet our own needs. "For a man who loves his wife actually shows love for himself" (Ephesians 5:28b). How are we to love our wives? By giving up our lives for her. And God tells us that when we do this, we are loving ourselves. He says this is the best way. The question is: will we trust Him?

I dare you to try it. If you don't believe, then believe your experience. For the next half dozen times you go to have sex with your spouse, put her needs first and foremost in your mind. Yes, it is still okay if you climax, but this is not the goal. This is what culture has taught us. This is what we may have learned through adolescence and young adult years—sex is about me feeling good. But this is not the goal. This is not God's goal! So change the goal! The goal is now for our spouse to enjoy the experience. Give it a try and see what happens. God's way of bringing us joy and delight is always through the joy and delight of others as we use our freedom to serve them in love. Apply it to sex, and suddenly God's plan will seem amazing!

THE LINCHPIN

You were made for relationships. I don't care if you are an extrovert or an introvert, shy or expressive. At the root of every human being is the need to know and be known, to love and be loved. Who we are as persons can never be defined through accomplishment, skill, or even character alone, but always in connection to the relationships we have.

When we live in secrets, denial, or deception, we accept a kind of half-life in every relationship. We want enough of the true love and friendship we desire to keep each relationship alive, but not so much as to experience the joy and peace God intends for every relationship, including our relationship with Him. Intimacy is the result of being fully and completely known, and loved still. When we experience intimacy, we are free to be who we are. This is the gift God gives to us and the gift we are designed to share with others. In the marriage relationship, this is also the basis for really good sex! These are the good gifts that God wants to give. No matter how far we have strayed, or how many times we have turned away from the Giver, God still longs to give to us as He did to Gomer and as He did to Israel.

In order to receive these good gifts, we must choose the path of true intimacy: facing the painful truth of who we are in the presence of others, and then, in honesty, discovering the grace of forgiveness.

This includes you who were once far away from God. You were his enemies, separated from him by your evil thoughts and actions. Yet now he has reconciled you to himself through the death of Christ in his physical body. As a result, he has brought you into his own presence, and you are holy and blameless as you stand before him without a single fault. Colossians 1:21-22

CHAPTER EIGHT | TRUE COMMUNITY

What does a sex addict look like? The term itself conjures up images of real sleazebags that slink in to covert addiction meetings under the cover of darkness. When Dr. Ted Roberts required me to join a For Men Only/Pure Desire recovery group, I will admit that this picture still had more than a little of my imagination. I was certain that I would be the outsider in a group of guys very unlike me.

But this is the story of how a bunch of normal guys taught me about myself and changed my life.

I dragged my feet up I-5 to my first group meeting. Ted had given me permission to keep my identity as a pastor a secret if I so chose. He said what was most important was to process my story, and the workbook, with others who were on the same journey. Because he required it, I agreed to do it. But I was determined in my heart not to like it. I could be led to water, but no one could make me drink! I had said to myself that I would do the bare minimum for the group; I wouldn't invest, I wouldn't disclose any more than absolutely necessary, and I would be present in body, but not in spirit. I was determined to just float through the group experience, certain in my self-delusions that this group really wasn't for me. This group was for guys who had a real problem. (Remember, I started the group very early in the process, which means I was constantly downplaying my issue even then.)

I found the room where I had been told to meet the facilitator an hour before the rest of the group would gather. When I entered the room, I met Dan, a kind, clean-shaven, friendly, gregarious guy in his mid-fifties. He reached out his big bear hand and said, "Welcome brother; I'm so glad you're here." Dan is the kind of guy you can't help but instinctively like. He was extremely open and honest with me about the path of his own addiction and what had brought him freedom. I managed to keep my profession a secret for all of about ten minutes. In the accepting grace of this former pastor, I couldn't help but open up and tell my story as well. And Dan totally understood. I can't say what it did for my soul to tell my story to someone who so completely understood the journey. Dan listened and then promised me there was great hope if I would stick with the program.

In spite of all my self-made promises to stay aloof and distant from this group of strangers, I found that it simply wasn't possible. I realized very quickly that I had to either be in and change, or be out and stay stuck. Over the next eleven months or so, I met weekly with this group of roughly ten guys, with some coming and some going. There were old guys and young guys. Rich guys and broke guys. Athletic guys and those who were less athletic. Good-looking guys and those not so good-looking. Ordinary guys like me who wanted to love Jesus and be free from their destructive behaviors. These normal guys changed my life.

This was far more than an accountability group. Rather than meeting weekly to go around and ask the awkward, "Did you mess up?" question, we actually had homework. Each week, we did about an hour's worth of homework from Pure Desire's *Seven Pillars of Freedom* workbook. If a guy didn't do his homework, he didn't get to talk at that week's meeting. As addicts, we learn to shoot from the hip pretty well, so this rule kept guys from skating halfheartedly through the materials. We came each week with our FASTER Scales filled out, which is a helpful tool to get underneath the actions of our week.[18] This scale forced us to ask not "what did I do?" but "*why* did I do it?" (I'll explain this more later in the chapter.) We also made phone calls. Each week, we were expected to call three other guys from the group and update them on our FASTER Scale, as well as our commitment to change for that week.

About a month in, I realized that something quite amazing was happening. I was no longer dragging my feet up that road to our group; I was actually looking forward to going. This gathering became a place of acceptance, transparency, and growth. Week after week, I marveled at how our lives could look so different on the outside, but be driven by such similar deceptions and patterns of shame on the inside. When I wrapped up my time with these guys, I was very sorry to leave. These men had become my friends. They knew me better than some of my own family members; indeed, they had become like brothers.

But I had to leave in order to focus my efforts on launching a similar group in my church. When I was ready to make my public disclosure at church, Ted encouraged me to invite other men to approach me in order to help start a ministry for guys struggling with pornography. He assured me that this was the safest way to get the addicts to show up and get them to deal with their own issues so they could be part of ministering to others. He estimated that between seventy and eighty percent of the guys who came forward would be actively struggling with the addiction themselves. Six weeks later, when I launched the group, I reported to Ted that he was wrong. One hundred percent of the guys who had approached me were struggling themselves! And that's how Pure Desire launched in our church—with a recovering pastor leading ten fellow addicts. This was real ministry!

Like most pastors, I felt a pressing need to train more men for leadership in our church. But I chose to put leadership development on hold to focus on the Pure Desire process. One night I looked around the circle of our new group and realized that every man I would have approached about leadership development was sitting in that room with me! I wanted leaders to train as elders. But all the leaders came to get free of porn. Imagine the pain I would have caused if I had tried to do this the other way around! Had I put these guys in leadership training, they would have felt the need to look the part and push their addiction even deeper. Instead, they found a safe forum to process their deepest needs and hurts. One night as we met, God whispered to me, "This is the best leadership training you could ever do!" I smiled and agreed. I now trusted and loved these men more than ever before. God was training an army of leaders for our church and our community. And all this was happening because I had chosen to own up to my weaknesses and sin.

On another occasion, I was processing the journey I had been on and I said to my group, "I feel like God has done more through me in the last six months of our group meeting than He has done in the previous ten years." They all shook their heads in agreement. "Oh, thanks!" I thought, "Just affirm my previous ten years of futility!" But that wasn't the case at all; they were simply agreeing with words of Jesus in Scripture: "My power works best in weakness" (2 Corinthians 12:9). My journey through pornography had finally gotten me out of the way so Jesus could do His thing in our church.

I continue to meet weekly with a group for friendship, encouragement, accountability, and support. And I wonder: *When did this become my favorite time of the week?* Because it is. I would have punched you in the nose two years ago if you had said I would look forward to a *weekly, two-hour* meeting, *with homework*, that required me regularly to share my weaknesses, fears, and sins, both past and present. I was so over-busy and overcommitted prior to this journey that I could not even see a free night for such a group. I joined because I had to. But what I encountered was the first small group where I actually saw and felt change, both in me and in others. I have sat through more than one small group in the past where I checked the clock every few minutes, longing to be done. With this group, time flies. Why? Because we are real with each other, and through this, God is doing something very real in all of us. He will do the same in you!

Warning: Not everyone stayed. I want you to know that in my experience, I noticed that some guys who seemed to need the group the most were also the most skeptical and hesitant to trust. A guy would come and tell his story, and I could see immediately the deep lies he believed and the deception that was ruining his life. He would come for a week or two, but when the time came for him to really dive in, he would jet out—disappear. My conclusion is that the deeper our issues, the deeper our fears of addressing those issues. We want the easy way out or the quick fix, so when we see that the solution is actually a long road of honesty, trust, and hard work, we balk at the idea.

GOD'S STORY: COMMUNITY ON DISPLAY

One of the side-struggles that an addiction can create in our lives is the inability to feel comfortable in a small group. We get so caught up in the hiding, the pretending, and the glossing over of glaring faults that we wrestle with the honesty and truth required for healthy community. Add to this that most small groups or communities unwittingly create an environment of comparison and status-keeping. The individuals who come look around the circle and decide how they stack up spiritually with others. They long for acceptance and belonging, so fitting in to the general mold of the group becomes more important than sharing weaknesses. When someone does plunge into the deep waters of their life, the group can become stiff and silent, unsure of how to react to such an admission, even when they could be saying the same things.

In order to break through into community that can transform, we must develop a new paradigm for how change occurs. This paradigm shift occurs when we understand the point of Jesus' parable of the runaway son (Luke 15:11-32).

You may know the story well, but let's rehearse the details for a moment. Jesus tells the story of a wealthy, prominent father who has two sons. One day, the younger son comes to the father and asks for his inheritance. We may not pick up on this in our modern context, but there are at least three problems with this request in the minds of Jesus' original audience. First, inheritances at that time were primarily land and slaves (not money) and therefore hard to divide. The holdings were generally kept together as an estate. Secondly, this estate would be passed down to the oldest son. Birth order was very, very important and it was not uncommon for the eldest son to get the whole estate, while subsequent sons received nothing. And third, the inheritance system of the first century was a "death-only" policy. Children inherited their parents' wealth when Dad and Mom kicked the bucket. For the younger son to ask for his share early is an affront to the relationship he had with his father, saying in essence to him, "You are dead to me already."

In order to fully comprehend this story, we need to be appropriately shocked at the father's response, as the first-century crowd most certainly would have been. "So his father agreed to divide his wealth between his sons" (Luke 15:12). We learn about the gracious, generous heart of the father in this decision. He is willing to do for his son what culture and customs of his day did not require.

One would think that because of this incredible gift, the younger son would take his stewardship of the father's good gift very seriously. Not so. The young man headed out of state and began to live it up. He squandered what was likely a significant sum of money on "wild living." He buried his inheritance in booze and babes until there was nothing left. He wound up so destitute that the only job he could find was feeding pigs, a despicable occupation for a Jew who would have viewed the animals themselves as defiled and unclean. In this low place, he was ready to eat the pigs' food if only someone would let him!

How this parable touches on our story! We have taken the good gifts of the father and wasted them away on self-fulfilling pleasure and fantasy. We run away from a good place and end up in a place of isolation and desperation, where even a small morsel of goodness in our lives again sounds incredibly appealing.

Like we may have done in our low place, the prodigal son began to devise a way to deal with the problem—a way out and a way back. He decided that living as a slave of his father would be a better living than his current experience. So he dragged himself back down the road to home. He had left with the dream of owning the world and he returned with meager hope of filling his grumbling belly. Imagine for a moment the shame he must have felt. His father had graciously given him far more than he deserved, and he had absolutely wasted it. And he knew it. As he plodded along home, he rehearsed his speech, "Father, I have sinned against both heaven and you, and I am no longer worthy of being called your son. Please take me on as a hired servant" (vv. 18-19). He doesn't deserve to be a part of the family any longer, but maybe he can hang around the edges as a slave. Have you ever felt this way in God's family? You feel that your stuff disqualifies you from really worshipping or serving like everyone else, but maybe you can stay close enough to the holy crowd to at least reap a few side benefits of God's blessing.

While the son gathered up the guts to grovel, the father was pacing the dirt road out front of his villa. The picture suggests that the father knew this would happen—that his son would destroy his life. The father could only hope his son would find his way back home before it was too late. When he spied the form of his wayward son cresting the horizon, he began to run. "And while he was still a long way off, his father saw him coming. Filled with love and compassion, he ran to his son, embraced him, and kissed him" (v. 20). The son's head was filled with shame, but the father's heart was overcome with love.

This was not the reaction the son expected. Even so, he launched into his speech, "Father, I have sinned against both heaven and you, and I am no longer worthy of being called your son" (v. 21). But before he can even complete his speech, the father interrupted. He called the servants and commanded them to put work away for the day and throw the good steaks on the grill. "Clothe him, feed him, let's have a party!" commanded the father. He wrapped his arm around his young son and accompanied him through the gates of his estate. The son had expected to walk through those gates under a cloud of anger and condemnation, but instead he was escorted through them in the loving embrace of his father. In his presence, everyone on the estate knew that the son was fully forgiven and free to be a son in the father's home.

As this story relates to our journey, I see five significant elements of the parable worth highlighting. The first element is that the son chose to return to the father. No matter his motives or schemes, the son made a significant decision to head back home; this was a choice to face his fears and the shame that he felt. This leads directly into the second element, which is the son's decision to humble himself. He could have attempted to return with the same bravado he exhibited when he had left. He could have tried to slide into his bedroom late one night and act like nothing had happened. He could have lied and said that he had a successful business out of state and had just returned for a visit. But the time for lies had passed, and the son returned with a humbled, repentant heart.

In our turning to the Father, we must make these same choices: We must choose to return and humble ourselves. God will never force us home. God will not make us be humble. In choosing to return in humility, however, we open up our lives to God's activity.

The third element of Jesus' story that we need to see very clearly is this: The father chose to humble himself. The father could have written the son off as dead. The father could have demanded full repayment of the inheritance. Instead, he let go of his rights and loved the son in spite of his failures. And in the ultimate show of humility, the father chose to run. This is the fourth element we need to highlight. He was more than just gracious, though to be gracious would have been more than enough. So filled with love and compassion was he that he sought the return of his son.

My friends, this is the heart of *your* Heavenly Father. I don't know what image you have of God—judge, angry parent, aloof deity—but this is the true Father as displayed through Jesus Christ. When we choose to return in humility, the Father runs to us with grace and forgiveness. He pursues us, and runs after us with love and compassion. We must never lose this picture of God! Author Simon Tugwell has expressed this truth so well:

> So long as we imagine that it is we who have to look for God, then we must often lose heart. But it is the other way about: He is looking for us! And so we can afford to recognize that very often we are not looking for God; far from it, we are in full flight from him. And He knows that and has taken it into account. He has followed us into our own darkness; there where we thought finally to escape him, we run straight into his arms.[19]

So great is the Father's love for us that we have run into His arms even without trying. We thought we were running from our addiction. We tried to run away from our fears and failure. We were running just to make our wives or others happy. And somehow we ended up in a bear hug from the Father who had been waiting for us all along.

The fifth and final element of note in this story is the father's celebration. The father does not celebrate because the son has achieved or accomplished something. The party is not starting because some financial gain has been made. The father calls for an all-out celebration simply because his son is home. The value is *all* in the son, just because he is a son.

We live in a day and age where people are not truly celebrated. Oh, for certain, when we see a celebration, a person is in the middle, but notice the reasons we celebrate. The success of a movie career. A championship won. The enshrinement into a Hall of Fame. Records set, years of successful employment and monetary gain, milestones reached. We celebrate people for what they have *done*.

Not our Heavenly Father.

He celebrates people for who they *are*. When you return to God in humility, you may not feel like you have much to offer— few accomplishments, little success. In fact, you may bring to God a litany of failure and disappointment. But what does He do? He throws T-bone steaks on the grill and makes all the angels stop working in order to come and party. A son has come home. You have returned, and you are valuable because you are, and always will be, a son.

THE PURPOSE OF TRUE COMMUNITY

By now you might be asking the question, "What on earth does all of this have to do with community and being in a small group?" Great question! Let me pull the loose strings together. I have been told that several other religious traditions have their own version of the prodigal son story. A young man takes his inheritance early, blows it in a foreign land, and returns in disgrace to the father. The other traditions, though, tell this story with one significant change. At the end of all the other stories, the father is stern, demanding the son work as a slave until his debt is paid. The father requires the son to earn back his place at the table. "Sonship" is not an inherent gift, but it must be earned through the ability to live up to a standard and please the father.

So let me pause and ask you: Which picture of your Heavenly Father have you been operating under? Do you see God as disgruntled and disappointed in your sin? If so, you will forever play the role of the indentured servant who must work off his debt in order to be free and buy back his rights. Or, do you instead see God as the Father who looks down the road, eagerly longing for His son to come home, and when He sees the son returning, He runs like mad to embrace this weary sinner with love and compassion? Only when you see God like this will you gain, through His Spirit, the power to be free. You can never become a son by working hard enough and living perfectly enough. You can only be a son by the free gift of God's grace.

This, at last, is how true change groups differ from traditional accountability groups. As I have mentioned before, accountability groups that deal with lust and pornography tend to be performance groups: Live up to the standard, work your way into change, prove that you belong. But this is not God's way! God's way is to come along and call us sons. No standard to live up to, no proving to be done, and no amount of work possible to atone for what we have done. Instead, we trust what God has said about us, because, "In an atmosphere of security and trust, persons are likely to be more ready to change. The child who trusts the mother lets go and takes the first unaided step."[20]

God calls us sons because He believes, He knows, that change comes from sonship, not through indentured servitude. *True community exists for us to remind one another that we are sons!* We are loved by the Father and are full citizens of His estate. This is the New Testament gamble that God has always made—tell them who they are, get it deep enough into the core of their being, and they will actually start to live like it's true.

When our Pure Desire groups meet, their primary goal is to help every man rediscover his standing as a son before the throne of Father God. When a man gets honest and confesses his sin, we thank him for his honesty and remind him how God feels about him. We embrace him with love and forgiveness, because it is through us that God now embraces His sons. We are the physical manifestation of a seeking, hugging God toward one another. All of the work that we do—all the homework, and phone calls, and FASTER Scales—comes out of our standing as sons. We are learning to be sons as we do the work that we do. This is very different from earning our spot. God has given us our spot already, and from this place of security we can learn to walk and live in freedom.

OUR STORY: GROUP THINK

Before you start to think that all these change groups do is sit around and tell one another about the grace of a loving Father (though this in and of itself would be immensely valuable!), let me walk you through six components of a group like this. All of these components are done under the grace of God as His sons. Even in these actions, we are trusting God to do the work. We are attempting to put into practice Paul's words of Colossians 1 and strive with all our effort even as we depend on His Holy Spirit at work in us.

The first component of a healthy change group is a thorough understanding of the power of your brain. Your brain is composed of over one hundred billion neurons, the same number as the stars in our galaxy.[21] At any given second, there are more than five trillion chemical reactions taking place between all of these neurons, with messages being sent through the body at speeds of more than 260 miles per hour. You are incredibly complex! And this complexity had a great influence over your inability to change in the past. Others may have told you to just believe God more, pray harder, and keep trying, but this didn't work because these actions, though important, fail to understand the power of neurological pathways.

Your brain is constantly creating neurological pathways. These pathways enable us to make decisions faster and easier by not having to devote as much attention to the task. If you pause and think about this, you recognize the brilliance of God's creation here. You get ready for work in the morning without even thinking about it, therefore giving you the freedom to focus on other things and work on other problems. Have you ever pulled into your parking place at work or into the driveway at the end of the day and realized you couldn't even remember the drive? This is a neurological pathway working on your behalf. But, as is always the case in sin, Satan has taken the beauty of God's design and perverted it for evil.

In the areas of lust and pornography, you have created these exact same neurological pathways, so that it becomes possible for you to head down that highway before you even realize you're driving the car. Your repeated behaviors have worked in the past to bring "relief" of your pain. Your brain learned that this method worked, and so the behavior became a learned pattern that was strengthened each time you chose that path. This highway became a four-lane interstate that began to trump even your core beliefs. The truth is that no circumstance or value in your life is more powerful than how God designed your brain to work, and under the influence of sin, that power has been warped towards sexual things.

Changing these routes can be a two-to-five-year process and that is the purpose of your group. As Dr. Ted Roberts explains, "New information alone will not help without a new community to get you off the insane highway you are on. Only friends who are fighting the same battle can help you get that noose off your soul."[22] Freedom comes through experiences and relationships, which happen in our group. Because we have been wounded through relationships, only through new relational experiences can we be healed! New experiences create new pathways. The new pathways become the lasting change you have been seeking all along.[23]

The second essential component to a group experience is learning to recognize the emotions and fears that are driving you. For too long you have been focused primarily on what you do. But what you do is driven by a *why*—why you do the things you do. What you do— the behaviors—can be pretty straightforward and easily identified, and therefore you are more aware of the "what." But why you do what you do—the emotions and fears behind your behaviors—can be trickier to spot. This is the value of your group and the weekly process of reporting to them through the FASTER Scale.

The FASTER Scale was developed by Michael Dye, a certified addiction counselor from California. In his work with drug addicts, he realized that he could predict a relapse into their addiction as far as six weeks in advance! After watching countless men and women progress down the same pathway, he believed there was a predictable pattern at work. This pattern became the FASTER Scale.[24] Amazingly, we descend down this path no matter what our struggle—drugs, pornography, gambling, food, you name it.

The "F" stands for Forgetting Priorities. We forget priorities, according to Dye, any time we start believing the present circumstances and move away from trusting God. Behaviors such as procrastination, preoccupation with material things, or having less time and energy for God and others show that we have moved into this first step.

The "A" stands for Anxiety and results from forgetting our priorities, which creates a growing background noise of undefined fear. In the change groups in which I have been involved, I find that most guys *live* in anxiety. This emotion is so commonplace that we have accepted it as our normal life experience. Guys are transformed when they identify this and embrace the truth that they don't have to live with anxiety! Anxiety is revealed through behaviors such as worry, using profanity, perfectionism, and fantasy.

The "S" stands for Speeding Up. As your body and brain experience anxiety, you try and outrun the emotion by going faster. This happens whether you consciously realize you're feeling anxiety or not. When you are super-busy and always in a hurry, unable to relax or slow down, feel driven, or find it difficult to stop and be with people, you're in the middle of speeding up.

The "T" stands for Ticked Off. You get angry when your methods of speeding up don't work. *Why don't others notice how hard I am working? Why won't anyone help me? Why doesn't anyone care that I am doing all the work around here?* These thoughts reveal your emotions, and you express them through overreacting, road rage, blaming or arguing—just to name a few. In this step, you're "getting an adrenaline high on anger and aggression," according to Dye.

The "E" stands for Exhausted. Truth be told, you can only stay in "ticked off" just so long before your body or your brain tires out and longs to give up. You start to crave methods of coping and feeling better. Coming down off of the adrenaline high created through the ticked-off stage, you open up to destructive all-or-nothing thinking. In this low place of physical and emotional energy, you're ripe for relapse.

The "R" stands for Relapse. "Returning to the place we swore we would never go again," in Dye's words. We cope with life the way we know how. It seems that God or others either can't or won't help us, so we help ourselves. Acting out results in greater guilt and shame, which actually strengthens the cycle and the possibility of ending up here again.

At the top of the scale, though is Restoration. We walk and live in restoration when "we accept life on God's terms, with trust, grace, mercy, vulnerability and gratitude," Dye has written in the FASTER Scale. Restoration means that we look at the life God has given us to live and we find contentment, joy, and peace there. We lean into relationships. We face our fears and identify the obstacles we are facing to freedom. The goal is to live daily in restoration, but the scale helps us to acknowledge when we have slipped away from that place.

Whether or not you use the FASTER Scale is less important than whether or not you learn to identify what is going on underneath the waterline in your life. Like an iceberg, the vast majority of your life is lived in your brain, out of public view. And what is underneath will eventually determine what comes up out of the water.

I have described the scale here so that you will begin to recognize how significant your thoughts and emotions are in creating your behaviors. You already know when you relapse; this step is pretty obvious. But are you aware of all of the thoughts, emotions and small choices that have led to that moment? Accountability groups, or performance groups, tend to isolate and highlight behaviors while a change group will emphasize and focus on thoughts, emotions, and the renewing of the mind.

The third major component of a change group is to assess and analyze the power of your story. This is the purpose of Pure Desire's *Seven Pillars of Freedom* workbook. (The *Genesis* workbooks use many of the same principles and are also highly effective for groups with mixed struggles or addictions. *Seven Pillars of Freedom* hones in specifically on sexual issues, while *The Genesis Process* invites each group member to identify their most significant struggle and work from there.) You may wonder about the need to do "homework" and write out answers to questions about your past. Why not just come in and talk about your life? This makes it too easy for you to hide or avoid certain questions. You will also miss significant connection points between your past and your present. Working systematically through your story engages your whole brain—the creative right and the logical left—in the recovery process. Change will not be possible if you only talk about what you are currently doing and struggling with. You must trace the path in your life; in so doing, you will rewire the pathways in your brain.

The fourth major component of a change group is committing to change one week at a time. I remember when I first began this journey in 2010. I was skeptical about my ability to change for the long haul. I was thinking to myself, *I'm doing fine now, but what about five years from now? I just don't know if I can make it that long.* My track record had shown an inability to change for more than brief stints. I mentioned this feeling to a counselor who said, "Can you make it through today?" "Well, sure," I replied. "Today is fine." He asked a follow-up, "And what about tomorrow?" "Yeah," I said, "I know I can do that, too."

"Then just keep stringing together days and they will add up to years," he finished.

Days adding up to years. Isn't this the true nature of all lasting change? Take the out-of-shape couch potato who wants to become a bodybuilder or a long-distance runner. A great week or two will do little to transform their sagging glutes and flabby gut. But weeks piled on top of weeks could produce the change they seek. No one week will get it done, but each single individual week is the most important one of all!

So also, your change will not come all at once. (Remember: two to five years to change the brain!) Change is the result of consistent effort in the same direction. This occurs in a change group by making weekly commitments to change. We end each of our group times this way: We identify the most significant factor driving us down the FASTER Scale, pulling our thoughts and emotions in the wrong direction, and we establish a change goal to address that issue.

Part of establishing the change goal is to identify the "double bind" that has kept us trapped. A double bind traps us because we feel stuck between a rock and a hard place; we are damned if we do and damned if we don't, so we stay where we are. For instance, if a big project at work is causing a man anxiety, he has a double bind. Facing the project could result in hard work, painful, long hours, and the possibility of failure or letting down a superior. Not facing the project could result in greater stress and anxiety, missed deadlines, and possible firing. Either way is painful. But identifying this bind enables us to choose which direction we will go.

Any significant area of your life where you have stagnated in change is the result of a double bind. A healthy change group will give you the ability to see the double bind and then establish a goal to choose the right thing, which, by the way, is usually the hard thing![25]

The fifth component of a change group is true accountability. I don't want you to think for a moment that I am against accountability. I believe it can be incredibly effective when done right. Too often, though, a guy will say to a friend, "You can call me any time and ask how I'm doing." When he does this, he puts the responsibility for change into his friend's hands, with the implication it is the friend's job to keep him clean. Change occurs when you put the responsibility to change squarely in your own hands. This is done in the group by committing to call three separate people and update them on your progress. You make the call and you choose to be accountable to others. I cannot tell you how hard we fight against this as men, but I can assure you that when guys get this, transformation takes off.

The sixth and final component of a healthy change group is learning to accept life on God's terms. This means that if you relapse or have a bad week, you can still show up at the group and own what you have done. As a man, you have learned well in other situations—particularly in church environments—that weakness and sin need to be covered over or ignored. When you do this, you're living life on your terms, or other people's terms, and so you must work hard to prove yourself or live up to the standards of others.

Accepting life on God's terms gives you the freedom to embrace the title God has already given you—beloved son—and live out of that truth no matter how well or how poorly you have performed during the week. What God has said about you is truer than anything else, and when you get this truth deep into your soul, you are free to be honest about failure and receive God's love and forgiveness through others in your group.

If you're reading this book and are already involved in a group of friends or peers—other guys on the journey with you—I highly encourage you to assess whether or not these components are present. Are you functioning in essence as a performance-oriented, try-harder group, or have you embraced that change comes through sonship? Are you intentional about reminding one another that what God says is the truest word of all? You could incorporate all of these ideas into your next meeting and see immediate results in your group dynamics.

If you're reading this book, however, and you think the book alone will be enough to get you free, then please do me a favor. Walk over to the nearest trash can, place the book inside and shut the lid. It will do you as much good in there as it will to read this in isolation. You got into this mess alone. You will only come out in community. If you're not willing to trust others with this journey, you will never be free because trusting others is actually how we learn to trust God. (I first read Dr. Ted Roberts' book,

Pure Desire in 2000, ten years before I started to change!) So find a group. Puredesire.org has a list of churches currently hosting groups. Chances are that a church near you is offering a similar kind of group if you would just do a little work to find out about it. Or start your own group. How? Open up to the one or two people you trust most. Chances are good that your honesty will provoke their honesty over the same issue, and the two or three of you could become a force that transforms your city.

THE LINCHPIN: WHY MATH IS OUR FRIEND

Satan can only trap us one at a time. He gets us away from the herd and destroys us in our shame and isolation. We commit sins and then hide out in secrecy, fearful of what others would think if we told the truth. We look around at church and see other happy, well-adjusted men and assume that we alone are the weakling who can't get his act together. But we are not alone. Statistics would even say that we are in the majority of Christian men—sad but true! But so long as Satan can keep us alone in our shame, he wins.

Here is the awesome truth: God sets us free in community. We are released from sin and shame in the context of groups, which means we have the exponential curve working in our favor! Satan can only trip men up through addition, one at a time. God operates in multiplication. If three men gather and each go out to influence one more, they will have six. Six become twelve, the twelve become twenty-four. You get the picture.

We cannot change alone. But God, through others, can do what we most desire. We must choose to trust, to be real, and to believe that the journey is worth the frustration and pain. The outcome is beautiful—just what we have always wanted, to be fully and finally free. Our healing is always bigger than us. It will affect a group, a whole church, even a whole community.

It's time to rise up and turn the tide in our cities and in our country. Now is the time to begin reproducing the grace and truth of Christ into the hearts and lives of men everywhere.

No more adding to the sad statistics of men lost in pornography. It's time to multiply!

> *Two people are better off than one, for they can help each other succeed. If one person falls, the other can reach out and help. But someone who falls alone is in real trouble. A person standing alone can be attacked and defeated, but two can stand back-to-back and conquer. Three are even better, for a triple-braided cord is not easily broken.*
> Ecclesiastes 4:9-10,12

CHAPTER NINE | BECOMING A MAN

The current reports and statistics on men in America paint a clear and telling picture. The average age at which a man marries is going up. The average age before he leaves home is up. The average age of men playing video games is up. The average professions a man will have by the age of forty is up. The average number of years his first marriage will last is down. The average number of kids he will have is down. The average number of organizations he commits to is down. What does all of this tell us about men? We live at a time when boys don't know how to become men. Our society is filled with men living out a prolonged adolescence in one form or another: at work, with entertainment, or in relationships. I am not afraid to admit that for quite some time, I was one of these stats.

Many others have done in-depth research and analysis on the juvenile state of men in our country. I won't attempt to duplicate or better their efforts. What I will do is take some time to honestly assess God's vision for authentic manhood. His ideal may be much different than you have imagined. But before we get that far, we need to clear away some thick fog that has accumulated on the lens of manhood, so we can see clearly what the Creator had in mind.

Much of my struggle with pornography revolved around misinformation of what it meant to be a man. Maybe I shouldn't say misinformation as much as a lack of information; in the absence of solid footholds leading to manliness, I charted my own path based on a severely flawed definition. This path began in high school as I observed the culture of the cool and popular guys at school. Most of them drank, went to parties on the weekend, and as far as I knew, slept around with girls. The kind of stories I heard in locker rooms or on football bus trips sounded so Hollywood-like; I found it hard to believe the girls I knew were actually involved in relationships (and behaviors) like that.

While I was generally an outgoing and social kid, I was shy when it came to girls. I knew how to be their science lab partner or joke about a math teacher over lunch, but I felt awkward with anything beyond that. I was also a "Goody Two-Shoes" church kid and had developed enough of a conscience that I honestly didn't want to behave like the boys I knew. But what I did want was the popularity, confidence, and stature that I perceived they had. I was mildly talented at the activities I undertook, but this success failed to deliver the level of esteem for which I longed. I longed to feel cool, tough, risky, and above authority like them. I felt like a little church boy in the presence of these "real" manly guys.

That is, until I discovered pornography. Viewing porn, and then holding this secret, did something in the part of my soul that wanted to measure up to the guys around me. They may have had their wild parties and their one-night flings, but I had all the women on the pages of my magazine. In those brief moments of acting out and giving in to my old self, I felt control, mastery, and desirability. In a word: manly—or at least my warped, culturally-saturated definition of the word.

I had a secret, which made me risky, edgy, and dangerous. *You don't know all of me!* I found myself thinking whenever I felt diminished by others. I had the "affection" of women. I had something in my life that felt illegal and wrong, things that I was too scared to be or do in other places. I was a rebel in my own mind. I was cool. I was dangerous. I was trapped.

Particularly in this area of manliness—of our identity—pornography creates an intense double bind. This double bind is a prison that keeps us locked up. On the one hand, the secret life of viewing pornography made me feel as if I had control, mastery, and desirability of women, at least for a few brief moments. But on the other hand, the very same action would leave me feeling controlled, mastered, and undesirable to anyone at all. I was left feeling manly, while at the same time feeling like my entire sense of personhood had been destroyed. What was even worse is that I continually craved this prison where I would feel both a rush of significance and a debilitating blow of guilt and shame. In a single instant, pornography would define who I was both positively and negatively.

What developed in high school did not stay in high school. We have a way of carrying with us any part of our lives that remains immature or undeveloped. These subsets of our thinking and acting do not merely drop away or phase out as we age physically. If we are immature in any area of our thinking, that immaturity will remain with us until we learn to grow. For me, this meant that I took the same manner of defining my manliness into college, marriage, and career. Manliness was always a product of measuring up to others in my world and being accepted by my peers as an equal. Anytime I felt lacking, pornography was always there to buoy me up again.

Where this left me was in a continual, deep cycle of trying to measure up. In college, every athletic contest was a chance to put my manly toughness on display. Every test or paper was a submission to have my intellect affirmed. In ministry, every sermon, every meeting, every counseling appointment became a litmus test for how well I stacked up to the men around me. The vicious left hook of this cycle is that it was never enough. No matter how much I accomplished or how well I did, the bar would just move up a few inches higher, seemingly always beyond my grasp. On my worst days, I felt like a failure. But because of this cycle, I usually felt like a failure on my best days, too.

This is the prison men all over our country are facing. We are running like crazy after an ideal of manhood without any clear idea whatsoever of where the finish line might be. Fearful that others may reach it first and leave us in the dust of their glory, we push all the harder to measure up and succeed. Welcome to insanity! Like greyhounds chasing the rabbit always before them, we pursue an unattainable goal.

This leaves us with two choices. One, we give up. We quit the race for manhood, give in to whatever feels good, and stop caring about what kind of impact our lives could have. The other choice is to redefine manhood. What if our sense of manliness came from God Himself? What if our identity as men had little or nothing to do with what we did or accomplished? As strange as that might sound culturally, this is God's definition. Let's dive into Scripture and I think you will see what I mean.

GOD'S STORY: HEAD AND SHOULDERS ABOVE THEM ALL

Allow me to introduce to you one of the manliest men in the history of the world. Manly by which standard? I will let you decide. In the Old Testament, God delivered the children of Israel from slavery in Egypt. They crossed the Red Sea and eventually made their way into the Promised Land. Through the power of God's hand, they drove out the inhabitants (mostly) and established themselves as a new country. For a time, the twelve tribes of Israel were loosely connected and governed by a series of judges—heroes who would rise up and deliver the people from foreign oppression.

After four hundred years of cycling between godly judges and subsequent times of general lawlessness when everyone did what was right in their own eyes, the people began to look around at the other nations. At that time, Samuel was judge over the tribes and he was about to appoint his two sons to succeed him. The people gathered together, though, and approached Samuel with the request for a king. "You are now old," they said, "and your sons are not like you. Give us a king like all the other nations have." (1 Samuel 8:5)

Samuel warned them that a king would take their sons for his army, take their daughters for his palace staff, and tax their land and holdings to run his kingdom. But the people begged for a king: "Even so, we still want a king," they said. "We want to be like the nations around us." Notice that their strong desire for a king was rooted in comparing themselves to other nations. The standard of leadership here was not God, but the status quo.

In spite of the people's flesh-based desire for a king, God conceded to their request and let them have a king. God sent a young man to the front doorstep of the prophet/judge Samuel. This was Saul, the clear choice for king. The Bible describes Saul as "the most handsome man in Israel—head and shoulders taller than anyone else in the land" (1 Samuel 9:2). Almost makes you wonder if Saul, or one of his attendants, wrote this book of the Bible!

At any rate, when Saul showed up on Samuel's doorstep, the prophet told Saul about the grand plans God had for him and his entire family. He told Saul this wonderful news, to which Saul reacted, "But I'm only from Benjamin, the smallest tribe in Israel, and my family is the least important of all the families of that tribe! Why are you talking like this to me?" (1 Samuel

9:21). Saul sounded very Gideon-esque in his reply. His self-description as the little, unimportant guy stands in stark contrast to the Bible's glowing report on him. This is the first insight, though, into Saul's inner workings. Externally, he was the guy everyone looked up to (no pun intended). But, on the inside, he saw himself as a nobody.

Samuel proceeded to anoint him there on the doorstep as the first king of Israel, according to God's instructions. In the next chapter, Samuel gathered together all the people to recognize this new king. When the moment came and Saul's name was called out, everyone turned expectantly to see this heroic leader emerge. He was nowhere to be found. It turned out he was hiding in the suitcases. Can you imagine pulling the next president of the United States out of the Delta baggage claim line? But that is exactly where they found their leader.

The aged prophet/judge Samuel placed the new king before the people and proclaimed, "This is the man the Lord has chosen as your king. No one in all Israel is his equal!" (1 Samuel 10:24). Now there was a man! Chosen by God, head and shoulders above the rest, and without an equal in all the land. Who wouldn't kill to have those kind of accolades said about them? If there was ever a man's man who could do the job of king, Saul was the guy! This was essentially how Saul began, an odd contrast of having all the traits and skills necessary to run a nation but none of the inner courage or conviction. His reign would be a similar mixed bag: stunning victory and accomplishment accompanied by shocking failure and disregard for the God who had anointed him king.

In one of these mixed instances, Saul and his newly formed army had just routed a small band of enemy Philistines. This defeat roused the full force of Philistines to march on Saul and his men. So intimidating was this hostile horde that Saul's men trembled in fear. They waited alongside Saul for the prophet Samuel to come and offer the proper sacrifices to God before the battle. The Israelites had seen God defeat their enemies enough times that they knew it was foolish to head into battle without His covering and blessing.

But Samuel was slow in coming. Very slow. The men waited for seven long, agonizing days as the enemy amassed before them. Saul looked up and down his line and noticed an alarming trend. Men were disappearing; right and left they were laying down their weapons and heading for the hills. So Saul made a rash move and performed the sacrifices himself, contradicting the law of God. Just as the smoke was clearing from the altar, Samuel the prophet showed up. And he had a message for Saul: Since he had disobeyed God by making the sacrifice, his reign as king would not last. Saul put the pressure to win the battle squarely on his own shoulders, and when the pressure mounted, he lost sight of his trust in God. God rejected Saul as king because Saul rejected God as his King.

Much like us, Saul was a slow learner. God had commanded obedience, but when that obedience became inconvenient, Saul did his own thing. A short time later (1 Samuel 15), Saul and his men destroyed the Amalekites, but kept King Agag alive, as well as the best of the sheep and cattle. This was a huge problem because God had specifically commanded Saul and his army to wipe out the Amalekites and spare nothing. As it turned out, Saul had only half-obeyed, destroying what was worthless or of poor quality, while keeping the best of the loot for himself and his men.

Once again, before the dust of the skirmish had even had time to settle, Samuel showed up. God had spoken to Samuel in a dream about Saul's partial obedience and his full disobedience, so when Samuel visited, he pointed out Saul's error. Saul did what every man must do if his identity is grounded in his performance. In fact, you might see some of yourself in Saul's response (1 Samuel 15, my paraphrase). I know I do!

- He deceives: *I have carried out the Lord's command!* (v. 13)

- He denies: *We are going to sacrifice them to the Lord. We have destroyed everything else.* (v. 15)

- He protests: *But I did obey the Lord.* (v. 20)

- He blames others: *My troops brought in the best of the sheep and cattle and plunder.* (v. 21)

- He half-confesses and blames some more: *Okay, I have sinned—but I was afraid of the people and I did what they demanded!* (v. 24)

- He seeks forgiveness in order to get what he wants: *Forgive my sin and go with me to worship (in front of my troops).* (v. 25)

- He becomes angry and desperate: *As Samuel turned to go, Saul grabbed at him to try and hold him back and tore his robe.* (v. 27)

- He worries more about looking right than doing right: *Please, honor me before the leaders and before my people by going with me to worship.* (v. 30)

Tucked into this incredibly familiar pattern of how we tend to deal with our sin and shortcomings are some words that demand attention. Samuel delivers to Saul a stunning, stop-you-in-your-tracks rebuke that every single one of us needs to hear through the grid of our lives. This is the kind of statement that hits to the very core of our addiction, the root of all our striving as men. Samuel says to Saul: "Although you may think little of yourself, are you not the leader of the tribes of Israel? The Lord has anointed you king of Israel. And the Lord sent you on a mission and told you, 'Go and completely destroy the sinners, the Amalekites, until they are all dead'" (1 Samuel 15:17-18).

God anointed Saul, sent him on a mission, and gave him a command to obey. This was to be the source of Saul's identity. But Saul had put all of his faith and trust in himself and his ability. Saul looked like a king, and he believed the subtle lie that this is what made him king: keep looking the part. If he failed to look the part, he would no longer be the king. This led him down a path of behavior to do whatever he had to do to create, protect, and re-create that image. Underneath his facade, Saul thought little of himself. He was a man's man, a successful king in battle, and had the world in his hands, but behind the glittering image was a little boy still trying to measure up.

Samuel told Saul again that God had passed the kingdom to someone else: "The LORD has torn the kingdom of Israel from you today and has given it to someone else—one who is better than you" (1 Samuel 15:28). Better than Saul? How could that be? Saul was head and shoulders above the rest, the best man in all of Israel. Was this new king better looking? No! We know David, the next anointed king, was ruddy in appearance. Taller? No! David was the runt of the litter. A firstborn, natural leader? No and no! David had nothing to compare with the talents and strengths of Saul. He was simply a man after God's own heart— anointed, sent on a mission, and commanded to obey. David found his identity not in what he had and what he did, but in who God had made him to be and in what God had given him to do.

In the end, "The Lord was sorry He ever made Saul king of Israel" (1 Samuel 15:11, paraphrase mine). Though God had anointed and appointed, He regretted. Rather than go into the theology about whether or not God knew He was making a mistake (couldn't God foresee these problems?), let me simply say this: Saul failed because he didn't trust what God had said about him. This made God sorry.

Saul thought his place as king came from what he had—his possessions, skills, and appearance—and what he had done—win battles, save people, accumulate wealth. When in truth, he was king because of what God had given him and what God had done.

It is the same for you and me. We can either try to be men based on our own resume, accomplishments, and skills, or we can recognize that our standing as men comes from what God has given us and what God has done.

What has God given you? Your skills, your accomplishments, your gifts and abilities, the family and people you have around you—are they not all gifts from God?

What has God done? Called you His son, made you an heir in His kingdom, granted you the forgiveness of sins and eternal life, shed His very blood to cover over your guilt and shame. Could you ever possibly eclipse what God has already done? How foolish would it be to try and out-accomplish God?

Saul had everything he needed to succeed, everything except a right view of himself. Absolutely everything was undermined in his life because he could not see the truth of who he was. He could have enjoyed a long, enduring kingdom. He could have seen his children and his children's children sit on the throne, generation after generation. But all of this did not come to pass because Saul's head was not right. On the outside, he appeared to be a man. In his own brain, he was still a child.

Although you may think little of yourself…

Think about that for a moment. How do you think about yourself? You may not have the stature or the standing that Saul once had, but I am certain that you have a great deal going for you. Why do I know this? God made you. God gave you a mission. God gave you commands to obey, all because He loves you. Do you see it? Although you may think little of yourself, God thinks the world of you.

True manhood is a result of being completely under the rule of a God who has anointed, sent, and commanded us to obey Him. God makes the man. We run into trouble the moment we think the man makes himself.

OUR STORY: MANHOOD REDEFINED

As I wrote parts of this manuscript, I sat at a beach house overlooking the Pacific Ocean. One afternoon, a loud, rumbling noise came down the street toward me, and I looked up to see a large truck in front of my window. Emblazoned on the side of the truck in bright green and yellow lettering was the word "WOW!" The font looked like something straight out of a comic book—fun, snappy, and fresh. WOW stands for Western Oregon Waste. It was the garbage truck. Seems like these days, everyone is trying so hard to look good!

Having a right view of yourself is far more important when it comes to being a man. So long as you look to the world and the standards around you for manliness, you will have no choice but to keep chasing the rabbit around the track. You will continue believing the lie that maybe, just maybe, you will be the first lucky greyhound ever to catch him! You become like a garbage truck disguised by a clever paint job.

I have sat with man after man who has so much going for him, but he can't see it. All he can see is others around him. He is stuck in a relentless cycle of trying to compare his life to the lives of others around him. He plays what Gordon MacDonald calls "the midnight games."[26] Late at night, he adds up his pluses, subtracts the negatives, and figures out how he stacks up to his peers.

If you have bought into this ill-fated pursuit, you open up your life to all kinds of destructive behaviors in order to keep up the appearance of manliness. Saul disobeyed God to try and impress the men and keep his image up. I pursued images of naked women to feel good about myself. Maybe you have done the same. Maybe you have cut corners at work to try and look better than you really were. Maybe you took credit for someone else's work, or passed off blame that really belonged to you. Maybe you tell your wife one story and your buddies another. Maybe the guys at work know a completely different you than the people you see on Sunday morning at church. In a million different ways, pursuing a culturally driven ideal of manhood sets you up to live in darkness.

If you desire to walk out of darkness and live in the light of what God says, you must be willing to make some tough decisions. You must see that the journey to manhood is not in what you do, but in the way you think. You must get your head right!

In the weeks that followed my final foray into pornography, I began to compile a list of all the ways in which I was juvenile in my thinking. Because I thought little of myself, I had allowed these traits to continue inside. As I looked at the list, I wrote the words, "I need to grow up. I am behaving like a little boy when it comes to lust and pornography. I am trapped developmentally and I need to grow up and become a spiritual man." Grow up in my behaviors? Certainly, but as you will see, all the items on this list are rooted in a way of thinking. The following list represents the number of ways I had lived with lies in my mind, thus forcing me to hide.

LITTLE BOYS	GROWN MEN
Do what feels good	Have learned to wait
Want it right now	Do what is right
Make life all about them	Care about others
Guard & protect their stuff	Guard & protect their relationships
Don't make commitments	Honor commitments
Play games because they're bored	Play to refresh and recreate
Look because they are curious	Already know what they'll see
Claim they didn't know better	Know better
Need to be taught right & wrong	Know the difference
Limit behavior because of consequences	Limit behavior because of love for God and others
Avoid punishment	Own mistakes/set things right
Use/pick up/chase girls	Treat girls like ladies/ with respect
Experiment	Honor theirs & others' bodies
Lack discipline	Learn discipline
Think freedom is in many choices	Know freedom is the result of sticking with good choices
Want to try out all the ships int the harbor without really learning how to sail	Pick a good ship and master the craft

So how do we grow in our thinking? How do we move from "thinking little of ourselves" to thinking as God thinks? How do we embrace His version of manhood? I offer the following three choices we must make.

CHOOSE TO BE A MAN UNDER AUTHORITY

One of the great lies we may have adopted from our culture is that freedom is the result of being an authority unto ourselves. This may have been rooted in the American Revolution, where we "threw off" the authority of English government in favor of self-rule. But this is hardly the first instance, or last, of freedom coming as a result of removing the tyranny of others. World history is replete with such examples, and so is our past. We "threw off" our parents' authority when we left for college or the military. We "threw off" teachers' rule over us at graduation. In many cases, progression from one arena of life to the next meant removing ourselves from the authority that held us.

Perhaps it is from this that we have gotten it in our heads that we are most manly when we call all the shots in our lives and make ourselves the highest authority. If you want to see how ridiculous this idea is, though, just try giving that kind of "freedom" to the people around you! Do you want other drivers on the freeway operating under their own authority? Do you want your coworkers to follow their own best ideas? Do you want your kids to do what they think is best? Do you want the high school boy dating your daughter to follow his own standard of conduct? Hardly. If we can recognize in these few examples how necessary higher authority is, how much more should we embrace the rule of a loving Creator in our lives?

God has invited us to make Him our highest authority. He has given us a command to obey. We must arrive at a place where we settle in our hearts that this command, this rule, is always our very best choice—even when we can't see why!

Such was the decision some men had to make in the New Testament. Early on in Jesus' ministry, He came upon a boatload of his soon-to-be disciples who were fishing (Luke 5:1-11). Jesus, the preacher, told these seasoned veterans of the sea to head out to deeper waters and throw their nets overboard once more. The experienced fishermen knew that this idea was ludicrous; they had fished all night in prime spots without a single bite. Now a hotshot young rabbi wanted to give them fishing tips? But their reply was priceless: "Master, we have worked hard all last night and didn't catch a thing. **But if you say so,** we'll try again." Their response was to say, "We don't get it. Your words make no sense in our way of thinking. But because you have said it, we will do it." They willingly chose to put their lives under the authority of another whom they believed knew better than they did. The results speak for themselves—more fish than their entire boat could hold!

If you say so. Have you come to that place with God? If He says it, is that good enough for you? Until you reach this point, you will struggle mightily to be free of lust, pornography, and any other besetting sin. Your brain will be susceptible to the lies that maybe that route has more promise, more life, than God's way. If you want to be a man, you must be fully under the authority of God in your life, trusting at every turn that where He leads is the best way to go. We come under God's rule by reading His Word regularly, by gathering weekly with other believers to hear and embrace truth, and by submitting our will to Him daily through prayer. We choose to listen to the advice of mentors and walk in accountability with others. Real men have made the highest authority possible their authority.

CHOOSE TO BE A MAN UNDER CONTROL

After the lie of self-rule, the second most common lie we give into as men has to be the lie of choice. We think that a real man is free to do whatever he would like, so long as it is not illegal or detrimental to his own health. To impose boundaries or limits on a man's behavior beyond the law of the land would be a denial of his rights. We think real men are wild, untamed, and free to choose between endless options. So long as it is permissible, he has the freedom to do it. This is a huge struggle for us with pornography. We hear so many lies in our culture:

- "It's not illegal!"
- "It's not really adultery."
- "No one is getting hurt."
- "Boys will be boys!" (Interesting, isn't it, that we don't say, "Men will be men"?)
- "What's the big deal?"

It may be odd for you to realize that this kind of thinking is not new. In fact, it is so first century! For two thousand years, men have been susceptible to this kind of irrational, egocentric thinking. The Apostle Paul addressed these very same lies in his letter to the Corinthian Christians. Even in the church some were saying, "I am allowed to do anything" (1 Corinthians 6:12). In a sense, this was true. Paul himself had declared that Christ set us free from the power of the law and we are no longer slaves to sin. But these men were taking that freedom in Christ to an inappropriate level. Paul responded by saying, "…not everything is good for you.… I [you] must not become a slave to anything" (1 Corinthians 6:12). In this conversation, Paul was specifically addressing sexual immorality. What we think is freedom is actually setting us up for slavery.

Everything is permissible, but not everything is beneficial! Paul's warning here: Even things we are free to do may end up having mastery over us. A real man can identify the areas where he is weak or susceptible to mastery and then purposefully choose limits for himself. These limits make him no less manly; in fact, they do quite the opposite. Creating limits so that a man can keep focused and directed is the ultimate source of freedom. How many men have been tripped up and prohibited from doing what they were best at simply because they attempted to live without limits in another area of their life?

Do you realize that God created a world *with* limits? From the very beginning, Adam and Eve had limits—things they simply could not do. They could not eat of a certain tree. They could not be partners with the animals, only with each other. God's *perfect* creation came with helpful boundaries. How much more do we need these in an imperfect, fallen world?

In the *Seven Pillars of Freedom* workbook, Dr. Ted Roberts reports on a study done by two MIT researchers. These PhDs discovered that when men were aroused, their ability to make moral, rational decisions went completely out the window. They concluded, "Men's self-control when sexually aroused doesn't come from willpower but from avoiding situations in which one will become aroused and lose control."[27] If two secular academics can get this, I think we can, too.

This single thought changed my whole approach to lust and pornography. You and I were not made to have the willpower to avoid sexual sin when aroused. Do you hear that? You cannot become "tough enough" to avoid pornography when you're sitting at the computer alone, your heart rate is up, your inhibitions are down, and beautiful women are one click away. The victory is found in not being in that chair in that moment! I had always believed if I was just stronger in that moment of intense temptation, I could be victorious. I have learned that the secret is to not be in that intense moment of temptation!

So I have learned boundaries. I have adopted limits. At first I created them, but ultimately my wife and my small group helped the most. I came to recognize the power of procrastination in my life. Putting off hard work became a means for porn to get in, so I have boundaries about how I work and study. I have chosen to limit my use of the Internet, TV viewing, and cell phone use in order to be free to do what God has called me to do. I don't have Internet on my phone. It's not smart at all. As a friend once related to me, "If your iPhone causes you to sin, pluck it out!"

God has given us a mission in this world. If we want to be about that mission, we must create guardrails in our life that keep us moving in that focused direction. What limits do you need to willingly live under? And can you recognize that these limits do not inhibit you, but actually set you free?

CHOOSE TO BE A MAN WHO IS RESPONSIBLE

The final lie that must be faced to move from adolescence to adulthood is that men are free from responsibility. Think of the commercials you've seen that appeal to men. These men evidently go to the bar and socialize with friends, and beautiful women, a lot. In these depictions, work is something to be avoided or endured as a means to spending the weekend on your Harley or your boat. Being tied down with things like kids, a mortgage, and a steady job don't grab much of the advertising dollar! All of these commercials display adolescence, not adulthood.

True men shoulder increasing loads of responsibility as the width of their shoulders also increase. They can handle more and they take on more. Core to the decision to be responsible is the choice to be held accountable for *all* our actions, both success and failure. Many are eager to shoulder the accolades or promotions that come with triumph. Few are willing to step up and be responsible for their failures. This began in the garden when God turned to Adam to ask what happened, and Adam turned and looked at Eve. "She made me do it!" In that moment, Adam became less man and more child. We have done the same ever since.

One of the largest, and typically last, hurdles you must face in order to be free from pornography is a complete willingness to own up to your mistakes *and suffer the pain of the consequences*! Coming clean with your past mistakes is one level of honesty. Coming clean about current indiscretions is another level entirely. Owning up to current or recent relapse and failure breaks the binds these behaviors have on your soul. You then willingly submit yourself to the group for appropriate restitution. Remember the Old Testament idea of restitution I mentioned earlier? It is a price paid above and beyond the damage itself in order to communicate to yourself and others that sin is costly. This cost changes our lives!

The kind of restitution "paid" should be a mutual decision between you and your spouse or you and your small group. If you're married, it must start with her. The two of you must sit down and write a safety plan for your wife. This plan details the price that you will pay, willingly, for relapse. Perhaps two weeks without your computer. Maybe you sleep in the garage or on the couch for a week. Having to abstain from your favorite hobby for a month or lose your smartphone permanently are also common ideas. Keep in mind that this is not punishment, but a purposeful plan to create pain and discomfort for your brain. This is the kind of experience that creates change in your brain—change that will last!

(Note: For a more complete description of safety plans and how spouses can create them, see Pure Desire Ministries' *Betrayal & Beyond Workbook II*)[28]

A WORD ON BOUNDARIES

Creating strong and effective boundaries may be the greatest challenge I face in leading men through the Pure Desire materials. Something inside of us as guys just rebels against the idea of being limited. We want so badly to believe that we can change our bad behaviors and make better choices without really changing the circumstances present in our lives. We want to have our cake (TV, Internet, iPhone, whatever) and eat it too (be free of pornography). Our world has coined a word for when we do the same things over and over, but expect different results: insanity. It doesn't work! Remember—purity is not a process of making better choices in the face of extreme temptation, but in avoiding the situation that creates extreme temptation for you. Boundaries are the only way to get there!

Think of it this way. If you lived on a large ranch in Montana and you wanted to go out and catch some wild stallions, one of the first steps you'd take is to build a sturdy corral with high, impenetrable fences. That way, when you had done all the hard work of wrangling a few of those mighty beasts, you could keep them fenced in long enough to break them, to train them. If, in the process of training, the wild horses break free and run off again, you will have to divert your efforts back into capturing them. Instead of shaping them into a purposeful machine, you will be off in the woods trying to rope them and bring them back to the ranch.

In your struggle with lust and pornography in the past, you were a wild stallion. (Feels kind of good, doesn't it?) But you found that life in the wild was not all it was cracked up to be. God, through His providence and Holy Spirit, brought you into the corral. You joined a group. You got honest with your wife. Good. That was step one. But if you keep breaking free and relapsing into the same stuff, all of the effort you could be putting into change will be diverted into dealing with the mess created. It takes time (two to five years!) for your brain to change. You must give yourself and your brain sufficient space for this change to occur. Boundaries are that space. So err on the side of caution. Set them too high. Be too severe on yourself. Build fences that can never be toppled. You will never regret steps you take to become a tamed stallion.

Tamed stallion. Sounds kind of dull, right? I know: You want to be a wild stallion, unbridled and free. But think of it this way: You don't know the name of a single wild horse. Wild horses die wild, and alone. All of the great horses, the ones of whom you have heard, were extremely disciplined to their task—warhorses, racehorses, and the like. They were animals of extreme strength under absolute control.

God can only use the stallion that is submitted to His leading. You can be a wild stallion, wasting your strength on the desert wind, and then die forgotten and alone. Or you can surrender wholly to the Rider who has an incredible destiny for you and live a life of great impact. It is worth creating whatever boundaries you need to create, so that you can reach this God-birthed destiny.

So ask your spouse this question: "What would make you feel safe?" (Or ask your small group, if you are unmarried, "What do I need to do to be safe?") Chances are, she will mention things quite a bit beyond what you think is necessary. That is okay. That is good. This is building a high fence. And if she says, "Never watch TV alone," then you never watch TV alone. If she says, "Never go somewhere unless you have told me that's where you're going," then you make that choice. When you do this, she will begin to feel safe, which creates an atmosphere for rebuilding trust. Trust is what we turn to next.

THE LINCHPIN: YOU CAN ONLY BUILD ONE

Imagine with me, if you will, that one day I am driving home from my office in beautiful southwest Washington. As I do, I notice that a perfect lot of land—with a beautiful view of the river—has gone up for sale. Out of curiosity, I call the number on the sign and find out the property is available for an absolute steal of a deal. It would be criminal to refuse, and so I buy the land.

From there, I approach two separate architects about designing my dream home on the property. One architect produces a modern, clean-lined layout with contemporary features galore. The other shows me a very retro, log-style home with real classic charm. I take the two sets of blueprints home to think it over. After a week of going back and forth, I walk into the best builder in our city and plop down both designs in front of him. "I want both," I say, "Just build them together!" The dismissive laugh the builder gives me would be well earned. Any fool knows you can't build a dream house off of two different designs.

Any fool ought to know you can't build a life that way either. We will take our cues on what it means to be a man either from the world and society, or from God. Which blueprint are you following? You cannot build on both; one will overrule the other.

We are seeing the tragic results of the world's definition as men are chasing their tails trying to out-tough, out-earn, and out-sell one another. They posture and pose, constantly looking over their shoulder to see who is watching. Meanwhile, their marriages are crumbling, their children are running, and their faith is dissolving.

What we have yet to see is what can happen when Jesus sets hearts free and men emerge who are under His authority and identity, men who know that what they do can never secure who they are. With their identity sealed and delivered through partnership with God, they forge lives that honor the Giver and bless all those around them.

Partner with God and become the man God created you to be! Our churches are dying for the lack of good men. Our world is in desperate need of real men. Will you be one of them?

Keep me safe, O God, for I have come to you for refuge.
I said to the LORD, "You are my Master! Every good
thing I have comes from you." Psalm 16:1-2

CHAPTER TEN | LIKE A CHILD

"But I don't trust you!" These words were hard to hear from the lips of my beloved wife. We were about six months into our process with Pure Desire and everything was going well. But on this night, we had watched a movie where I hadn't turned my head away from a scene showing a gal in a low-cut dress. I didn't perceive the scene as overly provocative, so when my wife expressed her frustration, I said, "Why don't you just trust me to know when to look away?"

Somehow this image had tapped into the pain my wife had felt from years of my bad choices. In that moment, I felt her deep and continuing lack of trust in me. I wanted her to trust me. I wanted her to see the change that I was seeing in my thinking and then believe the words I was saying.

But her words were hardest to hear because I knew they were true. If I were completely honest with myself, I knew I didn't trust myself, either! At least not yet.

Jesus said that in order to accept His kingdom, to take part in the life God has for each of us, we must have faith like a child (Matthew 18:2-4). We need the ability to come before Him in humility and to trust God. A simple, honest, and innocent faith. This kind of faith is all about trust. We take the words and ways of Christ and, in simple trust, we make them the cornerstone of our lives. What I have come to understand about myself and my past as I've been on this journey is that ultimately I didn't trust myself because I didn't know how to trust God. The two are inseparable.

Can I admit to you upfront that this is the part of the journey where I most feel like I am currently traveling the path? The other chapters, up to this point, have felt more like stops along the way where I learned and made progress. From a place of experience, I have tried to call back encouragement to you: Keep on going, you can do it! This chapter, however, feels less like a destination or an attraction I have reached along the way; it feels more like an ever-present reality of life's journey—of my journey and yours.

The topic I want to zero in on here is trust. Trust is the kind of word that gets mentioned frequently in Sunday morning sermons and generally evokes little more excitement than a stifled yawn. We know we need to trust and be trusted, but the term itself is a bit ambiguous and hard to know when we have obtained it.

It is painfully obvious when trust is not present. We can feel when trust has been broken or betrayed. We easily identify the people we don't trust with our possessions, our children, or our lives. How, though, is trust created when it's gone? How do we learn to trust again? This is a crucial question because most of the significant trauma we faced as children created a lack of trust. The dilemma that pornography has created in our lives currently is a lack of trust toward us. So how do we rebuild trust?

Trust is pretty important. I know you may be most concerned right now with how to get others to trust you again. You have broken their trust and you want to know how to rebuild their faith in you. I will get there. But if we ever want to have others trust us, we must first be people who have learned to trust—most importantly, to trust God, but others as well. As we learn what it means to trust God and others with who we are, we can become the kind of people who are trustworthy.

Others will not be able to trust you until you have first learned what it means to trust others. Getting others to trust you is driven by a desire to remove the relational discomfort and pain that mistrust creates. You are uncomfortable because people don't trust you. But do you want to relieve pain, or actually change? Change, and true freedom, is the result of learning to trust again, not simply convincing others to trust you. If you want others to trust you, you must learn to trust God completely.

At the root of trust is the idea that no matter what happens, we can depend on someone being there for us. That person is consistent in their love and care for us, so much so that they always have our best interests in mind. Since this is the case, trust can be broken in relatively small ways. We don't have to have a parent walk out the door or a relative abuse us. Those instances, and many others like them, create obvious breaches in our ability to trust others. But the same emotion can be created in some of the routine of life.

Let me give a few examples from my own life. In school, I can remember an incident where some of my friends turned on me. In the fourth grade, there had been an all-out spit wad fight in our classroom every time the teacher turned her back. I had attempted to get involved, but didn't actually have the skill to make the spit wad fly. (Imagine the humiliation!) I didn't even have the skills to be bad. However, when the group was caught, I was implicated along with all the others. None of my friends was willing to say I was innocent; they were glad to see me pay the same price they did of writing one hundred lines, "I will not shoot spit wads in class." This instance taught me that even friends can't always be trusted. They may turn against you.

A few years later, after an intramural flag football game in the sixth grade, I had cried because my team lost. At lunch the next day, a group of boys pointed at me, chanted "crybaby!" and laughed together. I felt very alone and exposed in this moment, with no adult or friend there to defend me.

Later that same year, a couple friends and I discovered that the track shed didn't lock properly. In an hour of boyhood fun, we spread an entire bag of limestone chalk around the interior of the shed. (Limestone chalk was used to line the dirt track.) We were later ratted out and suspended from school for a day. Several kids I thought of as friends made fun of me and began to treat me differently after this. I felt angry and betrayed by those who should have understood, but did not.

In the grand scheme of life and loss, these stories are relatively small. No serious injury or lasting harm was done. But in each of these instances, I translated the experience on an emotional level into a deep decision about trust. Friends could not be trusted because they might turn against you when you did wrong. Teachers and authority figures could not be trusted because they weren't willing to take the time to really know you and find out if you were innocent or not. Parents could not be trusted because there would be times when they simply couldn't be there to protect or defend you. From these instances, and many others like them, trust in others—believing they had my best interests at heart—began to disappear.

Others may not have been consciously attempting to create this lack of trust. It has as much to do with how we *perceive* the situation as anything else. We read into an event on an emotional level and make decisions about how God, or others, can and can't be trusted.

Perhaps you could look into your own life and see that you have done the same. In stories from your life, examples both big and small, trust has been shaken. God didn't protect you. God didn't heal her. They didn't love you. He didn't pay attention to you. Dad wouldn't come to your game. Through all of this, you begin to fear failure, loss, and pain. "Who will protect and take care of me?" you begin to ask.

Sooner or later, we all arrive at the same conclusion: I will. If it has to be, it's up to me. The only person I can completely trust to be there for me is…me! So we stop trusting others and put ourselves at the center of it all. The only problem with this thinking is that we know what we do—we know our secrets, our faults, and our shortcomings—and we know we aren't worthy of that trust! And when we make this decision to trust only in our own self, others are unable to trust us. Trust will always be mutual; when we trust others, others can trust us. When we lack trust in others, we are led into behaviors and choices that make us the kind of person who is hard to trust.

The result of all this is anxiety. Anxiety is the emotion we feel as a result of fear. When we can't trust others, and we can only depend on ourselves, we have no choice but to be anxious about the situations we face in life. My need to perform in life came from deep anxiety, anxiety triggered by fear—fear of failure, fear of being insufficient or unprepared. Trace your anxious moments and you will find the same root; there is no one else to trust with what we are facing, so we feel anxiety about our ability to do what needs doing. We are anxious because of our fears.

Do you have any recurring dreams? If you do, I'm guessing that they can be traced to this same kind of anxiety. Mine is always the same. Actually, I have two. One is all about sitting in a boat, fishing for something mammoth, and then falling in the water. I have no idea what that one is about! But in the other dream, I am in some kind of church service or public gathering. In a panic, I realize that I am about to be introduced as the speaker, only I have no talk prepared. I begin this frantic process of scribbling out a few notes on a napkin or my hand to try and fake my way through a presentation. Should this dream come as a surprise when some of my most common fears are being caught unprepared or being embarrassed?

Fear and trust. If I don't trust you, the result is fear. If I don't trust God, the result is fear. And if others don't trust us, the emotion they are feeling is fear. These are two sides of the coin—one of which will always be driving our life and our choices. Either we trust God and live in peace, or we lack trust and live in fear. So how do we learn to trust again? How do we make sure that we aren't spending our lives reacting in simple fear and self-preservation? The answer is found in coming back to a topic that I touched on earlier in the book, but now I want to return to it in full force.

The answer is found in believing that what God says about us is true. His ways are always best. Receiving our identity from God is primarily an issue of trust versus fear. Will we trust that what God says is really, actually, completely true? Will we believe this about His Word? Most importantly, will we believe it about ourselves?

GOD'S STORY: FATHER KNOWS BEST

No character in Scripture displays for us this mix of trust and fear like the disciple Peter. In Matthew 16, Peter had been following Jesus for about a year and a half, roughly the midpoint of Jesus' ministry. Peter had heard Jesus preach some powerful sermons, watched Him feed the five thousand, and even witnessed the raising of a little girl from the dead. On this particular day, though, Peter and the other disciples were simply walking along the road with Jesus. As they did, Jesus turned and posed this question, "Who do people say that the Son of Man is?" (Matthew 16:13).

At first brush, Jesus appeared to ask a fairly straightforward question, but that was not the case here. This phrase "Son of Man" was actually first used in the Old Testament book of Daniel (Daniel 7:13); by the time of Jesus and His disciples in the first century, Jewish rabbis and scholars had all kinds of differing opinions about the phrase and who it described. On top of this, Jesus had, on occasion, seemed to use the phrase about Himself.

So don't blame the disciples if they appeared a little uncertain about how to answer. Jesus had a way of posing semi-vague questions to people and then zinging them with truth when they gave a less than accurate response. You can almost hear the hesitation in their voices as they responded (and I'm paraphrasing just a bit), "Well, uh, some say John the Baptist, some say Elijah, or Jeremiah." And then just to be safe and cover all their bases, they throw in, "or one of the other prophets. There you go, Jesus. That's about as vaguely specific as we can get!"

As He often did, Jesus took a vague, theological question and turned it into one very direct and very personal. "What about *you*?" He says, "Who do *you* say *I am*?" (italics mine). Jesus didn't want to know the theological viewpoints of the day. He was asking very pointedly what His followers believed about Him. Had the ones who watched Him most closely understood the significance of what they were seeing?

We might be tempted to think that by this time, the disciples should be pretty certain. They have had a front row seat to eighteen months of the Son of Man doing His thing and preaching His sermons. But the fact that Jesus asked in this way indicated that even now, they might possibly still misunderstand what He had come to do and who He was.

Not surprisingly, though, Peter stepped forward. While the rest shuffled their sandals nervously and kicked at stones along the road, Peter broke the silence and declared, "You are the Messiah, the Son of the living God." In other words, Peter was saying that Jesus was the long-awaited hope of Israel, and even more, Jesus was the Son of God.

The Messiah was more than just a person for the first century Jew. The Messiah for them had been prophesied centuries earlier, and had now become the focus of all their hopes. The Jewish people believed that when the Messiah came, all things would be set right. Jerusalem would be freed from Roman rule, Israel would return to national prominence and strength, the land would yield abundant crops, and the time of the Lord's favor would begin. The most significant hopes of every Jew hung on the appearing of the Messiah. So when Peter declares this about Jesus, he is saying, "You are everything we have hoped for and everything we need."

Peter nails it! Peter's answer displays that he had added all the pieces together and deduced that this young rabbi they had been following around Judea and Galilee was actually the long-awaited Redeemer of Israel and the Savior of the world. They had walked in the presence of God's Son.

Jesus replied, "Peter, you are blessed. You got this from God! No man could have revealed this truth to you" (Matthew 16:17, my paraphrase). And then, Jesus goes on to say something very interesting (again, some of my paraphrasing here): "Now that God has helped you see who I am and what I have come to do, let me tell you about who you are. You are Peter—Rock—and on this rock I will build my church, and hell itself won't be able to stop it."

The phrase "upon this rock I will build my church" has been hotly debated through the centuries. Catholics claim that Jesus was establishing Peter as the cornerstone of the future church. Protestants tend to claim that Peter's statement, "You are the Messiah," means that Jesus is the Rock. I do not hope to settle that debate in this book. What I would like to point out is the personal interaction here between Jesus and one of His followers.

When Peter made this declaration about Jesus, the first definitive statement we have from one of the disciples about their teacher, Jesus in turn made a definitive declaration about Peter. Peter, in faith, made a statement about the character and nature of Christ, and because of this recognition, Jesus made a statement about Peter's identity. Up until now, he had been Simon, but now he was Peter. And whether he was meant to be the cornerstone of the church or not, he did become a rock in the church, the bride of Christ.

Here is the truth we see in this passage: When we know who Jesus is, we can allow Him to tell us who we are. The two are tied together. One is not truly possible without the other. Recognition of Christ and His true role in our lives and in the world will always lead to a redefinition and understanding of who we are.

Even though Peter came to this stunning conclusion, he still had some work to do. Jesus had called him the rock, but that didn't mean he automatically became the rock. He had acknowledged the truth of who Christ is, but he still had to let that truth work its way down into his life. Peter still stuck his foot in his mouth and tried to dissuade Jesus from the cross because he misunderstood Jesus' true mission. Peter still whacked off the ear of a guy who came to arrest Jesus in the garden. Peter still denied Christ to a servant girl and then ran off to his old life of fishing even after Jesus had come back from the dead.

Each of these episodes from Peter's life is a sermon unto itself, but I want to make this overarching observation: What Peter knew to be true of Jesus (Savior) and what Peter knew to be true of himself because of this (Rock) transformed him only after he learned to *trust*. He had to fully trust that who Jesus was and what Jesus said were true.

As you may know, Peter did eventually get there. At the Sea of Galilee Jesus came to Peter and reaffirmed him as one of His disciples. It's interesting that this was also the location of his first call from Jesus. Jesus sent him into ministry to "feed His sheep." Peter watched as Jesus ascended to heaven, and he tarried with the other disciples waiting for the Holy Spirit to come. On the Day of Pentecost, when the flames of fire filled the hearts of the gathered believers, something had changed in Peter. This man who couldn't defend his friendship with Jesus to a teenage girl now looked out over a crowd of Jewish men and accused them of killing the Lord of Life. He told them that the blood of an innocent man was on their heads—bold words to a crowd that could easily turn hostile and do to Peter exactly what they had done to Jesus! Bold, but effective, as three thousand men come to faith in Christ on that day.

What had changed for Peter? If you ask me, the death/resurrection/ascension sequence of Christ together with the empowering of the Holy Spirit solidified Peter's trust. He now knew the true Messiah, the Lord of Life, and in this knowledge, he knew himself. He was finally free to be the Rock, to be the man that God had created him to be and that Jesus had recognized him to be from the beginning of Jesus' three-year ministry. Peter trusted and in so doing, he became trustworthy. And in this transformation, fear disappeared. His identity, and his life, was secure. In this security, he could be who he already was.

Understand this. Peter had been "let down" numerous times by Christ. He had in mind a Messiah that was coming to take names and kick some butt. He fully expected the toppling of Roman rule and a reinstatement of a free and powerful Israel. At numerous turns, this view caused him to slam headfirst into Jesus' plans to serve, die, and give His life away. Trust was not immediately present simply because he was in the presence of Jesus. Peter had to come to a place where he accepted what Jesus wanted to do *on Jesus' terms*, not on his own terms. Peter had to let Jesus be who Jesus was, not who Peter thought Jesus should be.

I have listened to many men who have a hard time trusting. A parent betrayed or abandoned them. A spouse cheated or left. A friend turned on them or a coworker undermined them. But underneath this lack of trust in others, what always surfaces is a lack of trust in God. God hasn't done what they believe He should do in their situation. In this belief that God should be God on their terms, they have determined that they can no longer trust God.

Freedom and restoration is a process of renewing our trust in God by accepting God on His terms, by recognizing that though we may not always understand what He does or what happens to us, God is good and He is for us. His plans for us are not to harm, confuse, or destroy us. That's what Satan wants to do! God, through His Son Jesus Christ, wants to give us life and life to the full.

Will you believe Him on His terms and fully trust Him? If you will, then He can speak over your life an identity that is true. Trusting Him for who He is leads to knowing yourself for who you are, which ultimately results in others trusting you as well. Let's talk more about how this happens.

OUR STORY: STANDING SECURELY

You need to know this about trust: Trust is not primarily about doing, or not doing, the right thing. Certainly, an error in judgment or a poor decision can break trust, but even so, behaviors are not the source of trust. *We put our trust in people, not in behaviors.* Therefore, restoring trust in your relationships is less about *behaving* the right way and more about *being* the right kind of person. The kind of person that you are—your being—always comes from your sense of identity.

If this is the case, then the kind of person we are becoming is far more important than any individual action. So long as trust is seen as the result of right behaviors, we must forever walk on eggshells for fear of losing trust. We develop lists and boundaries of right behaviors that we think will regain the trust of a spouse, a boss, or a small group. This can be so frustrating because we might do all the stuff on the list and still feel a lack of trust.

This is what my wife was expressing to me during the conversation mentioned at the beginning of this chapter. No matter how many things I did right, I felt as though the list was always longer. Why? Because my wife had determined I was an untrustworthy kind of person. She wasn't looking for any one behavior (or twenty behaviors) to decide she could trust again. She needed to know that I was transforming into a trustworthy kind of person.

Focusing on becoming the right kind of person is actually far more liberating. We trust God, not because at every turn He did exactly what we wanted, but because we believe He is trustworthy. Peter learned to trust by knowing who God is, and through that, knowing who he was. When he let God be God and he let Peter be Peter, he could live a life of confident trust and others could trust him. Whether he was meant to be the rock or his statement was the rock, Peter was part of building the church *because he was trustworthy*. His identity came from God and so God could use him for His glory.

Since trust is about a person, not a behavior, we focus our efforts on who we are and who we are becoming. Certainly, a number of right behaviors are highly significant in this change, but the behaviors are not the foundation. Our source of identity is.

Let me illustrate it this way. I would describe my life in the past as a circle in the middle with any number of smaller circles on the outside. The middle is empty and stands for my sense of identity. My core identity was blank, or empty. I was looking to all of the other factors in my life (the smaller circles) to define me. I was *doing* in life in order to find a center. In other words, lacking a true sense of identity, I walked into every arena of life hoping it would define me: relationships, sports, hobbies, even church activities and participation.

If you are in this place—expecting your wife, your kids, your job, your church, or any other number of things to define you— you need to see the danger in this kind of living. You see, none of these things can define you. They will never be enough. They won't be enough today and they won't be enough tomorrow. Feeling as though you are not enough, you will live and act in ways that break trust because you're grasping and striving for a center. You don't intentionally seek to be untrustworthy, but you have no other choice. You were made to have an identity, and if that core place is empty, everything will be twisted to try and meet this need.

Over the last few years, God has been establishing my identity in Him. I am recognizing that nothing I do, nowhere I go, and no one I know can possibly give me a higher identity than has already been given me in Christ. Trusting what God has made me to be gives me a center. When this identity is in place, I can walk into all the other arenas of my life as a trustworthy person. Having the center—my identity in Christ—firmly established, I can live with joy and contentment today. I no longer need these other factors to define and explain who I am, which leaves me free to be a blessing and an encouragement in all these places.

This is a place you need to find. You need to find that place where who you are—your identity—is settled in Christ. No matter what your situation, the Heavenly Father loves you with an intense, inescapable love. He knows who you truly are and is waiting to deliver this truth to you as you turn and trust Him. Making this choice frees you to live fully alive in today. Having received an identity from the highest place possible—God Himself—allows you to receive each day as a gift.

How do lust, pornography and sexual addiction play into all of this? These behaviors are more than just what breaks trust; these are activities we gravitate toward *because of* broken trust. In *Seven Pillars of Freedom*, Dr. Ted Roberts reminds us that sexual addiction is about an "attachment disorder or an intimacy deficiency."[29] This means that our acting out sexually is primarily about relational dysfunction. We fail to experience the trust and joy of a real relationship, so we give in to the cheap promises of false ones.

Relationships are all about trust, and trust takes time and hard work. Anytime we ask or expect someone else to define who we are, we will twist the relationship for our own benefit, resulting in us acting in ways that violate trust. When we don't trust God or others with our true selves, we run. And various forms of sexuality stand ready to receive us and give us a false sense of worth, peace, and victory. But none of this lasts, because only God can meet the deepest needs of our heart. Our heart is crying out for a Savior, but our brain will go after the quickest fix.

So how do we learn to trust God and others with our real selves? There are three environments that breed this kind of trust.

FEAR GOD ALONE
Scripture is filled with many passages about learning to fear God. I have often heard this word "fear" described as a kind of healthy respect and reverence for God. I tend to be a bit of a skeptic, so during my college years I started studying these verses for myself

in the original languages. The problem I found is that the word for fear used most commonly in Scripture doesn't mean healthy respect or reverence. The word means terror, dread, absolute panic.

How could this be? I thought to myself. The God I knew—the one I had been taught all about—was loving, kind, and forgiving. How could I fear Him? Unlocking this mystery somehow seemed key to understanding what faith is all about.

I finally got the picture I needed of what it means to fear God a couple of years ago on a hike. I use the term "hike" generously, because this was a real climb, ending with us harnessed to ropes, carabiners, belays, and the whole bit! I was on an excursion with a couple of friends on Three Finger Jack, a mountain in central Oregon. We were climbing with an experienced guide who knew all about the mountain and had personally summited this peak dozens of times.

Along the way, our guide Dave told several stories of people who had died on the mountain. He would point to a narrow spot on the trail and say, "That's where someone wasn't paying attention and slid 1,000 feet to their death." He directed our attention to a darkened scar on the face of the mountain: "That's where a small plane failed to observe the laws of mountain flight and crashed in a ball of flames." After numerous stories like this, my estimation of the mountain began to change.

Then we arrived at the part of the trail that was just us and the bare rock face. Not a fan of heights to begin with, I suddenly found myself clinging to the mountainside with newfound intensity. The mental images I had of Dave's stories began to flash through my mind, and I was determined to not become the next one. After what seemed like an eternity, we made it to the summit, which consisted essentially of a large, flat rock the size of a dining room table. Dave said, "You can stand up on it if you want, and I'll take your picture." So I did. Or, I should say, I attempted to stand. My legs were shaking so badly that all I could manage was a slightly heightened squat. The wind was whipping, and it honestly felt like a strong gust could blow me right off the side of the mountain and into the valley thousands of feet below.

On that day, I feared Three Finger Jack. Now that's an interesting statement because the mountain had no ill feelings or malice toward me. The mountain had no harm in mind for me. My fear was not rooted in a belief that the mountain was out to hurt me. But the sheer magnificence and power of something infinitely larger than me triggered very real fear in my brain. I was willing to do whatever the rules of the mountain dictated so as not to become an unsuspecting casualty.

I think this illustration strikes at the heart of what it means to fear God. His ways and His presence are so far beyond our own that we cannot think for a minute to treat Him casually. He has no ill will toward us, quite the opposite, in fact. But His power is so overwhelming and infinitely beyond ours that we willingly do whatever He requires. We trust Him because His power demands it. The fear we experience is real because we don't know how else to react in the face of someone so almighty.

Fear of God means that we are consumed with doing what He says above any other thing. When we allow this to get into our thinking, we begin to wrap our lives around His ways. Everything we do and say gets put in His light for evaluation. This transforms us into the kind of people who are completely trustworthy. As the book of Proverbs states, "Fear of the LORD is the beginning of wisdom. Knowledge of the Holy One results in good judgment" (Proverbs 9:10). His wisdom and understanding shape us into trustworthy people.

CONTENT YOURSELF IN HIM

The second environment that leads to greater trust with God and others is accepting that our best life is in Him. Failure to accept this was the root issue of the sin of Adam and Eve in the garden. They had a perfect world all around them. They had the best life God could give. But a sly voice slithered along and whispered, "God's holding out on you. He just wants to make you follow these rules because He doesn't really want you to experience life." The first couple took the bait, and we have been doing the same ever since.

We may be deceived to think, "God's standard of sex only within marriage is limiting and pointless." Or "Loving and serving my spouse won't really get me what I need." Or even, "Knowing God isn't really all that great." We listen to these lies and many others like them and then determine to pursue a better life on our own.

Trust is a decision to stop reaching for something beyond what He has given us already. We look at the life He provides and say, "We will live it!" We determine in our hearts and our minds that what God has for us, and what God asks of us, is always for our best.

TRUST BEYOND LOGIC

One of the greatest hurdles we have to get over is our brain. In addictive behavior, we have learned to trust only ourselves. In so many ways, we became the highest authority on all things in order to justify all our behaviors. Even as we come out of these impulsive behaviors, we may inadvertently hold onto this deficient way of thinking that says, "Unless I can understand it, it must not be true." We limit our beliefs to only those things that we can rationally and logically understand. I hope that when I state it this way, we can all see the foolishness. To place yourself—

your finite, rebellious, willful self—as the highest authority is a darkened way to live.

Trusting God means that even when we cannot see, we will trust the One who does. Even when we cannot see why something makes sense, why it works, or why it helps us, we will be humble enough to acknowledge that we are not the highest authority. God is. We don't know best. God does. The Apostle Paul says it this way in Romans 9: "Who are you, a mere human being, to argue with God? Should the thing that was created say to the one who created it, 'Why have you made me like this?' When a potter makes jars out of clay, doesn't he have a right to use the same lump of clay to make one jar for decoration and another to throw garbage into? In the same way, even though God has the right to show his anger and his power, he is very patient with those on whom his anger falls, who are destined for destruction" (vv. 20-22). We are clay and He is the Potter. Accepting this gives us freedom to be the best lump of clay we can be!

Some of what God says and does will not make sense to us. In humility, we submit ourselves to His ways and begin applying His truth in our lives. If we wait for all of God's commands to make sense before we act, we may wait forever. When we dive into truth even when it makes no sense, we will see the wisdom as it plays out in us.

This is one of the fundamental choices I had to make with the Pure Desire counseling process. I thought of myself as a pretty wise and intellectual person, so I was very tempted to dismiss parts of the process as unnecessary or pointless. But I also knew myself as someone who had struggled with pornography for fifteen years and had been unable to stop no matter how hard I tried. Change came into my life because I chose to trust that God had revealed truth to someone other than me! I had to submit myself to wise, godly counsel even when it didn't make sense to me, and God then used the counsel to change my life.

You also must make this choice. Trust God beyond your own logic, and the doors of freedom begin to open wide!

Creating these three environments in your life—fearing God alone, contenting yourself in Him, trusting beyond logic—will result in greater trust in God. He will be at the center of your life and will reveal your true identity. I love this simple Charlie Shedd prayer often quoted by Dr. Ted Roberts: "Lord, help me understand what You had in mind when You made the original me." I would add to that: "God, help me see myself the way You see me, and help me to become who You already know I am." As we begin to live out this prayer, we become trustworthy people whose behaviors can be trusted because they come from an identity grounded in Christ.

A WORD ON REBUILDING TRUST

Learning to trust God makes you a trustworthy person. This is a process, and trust rebuilds slowly. If you have broken someone's trust, you undoubtedly want them to hurry up and trust you again. You start doing all the right things, but still they won't trust you. Why? Because this is a process, and changing who you are takes time. Changing the emotional impact you have had on others takes time.

Think of it like this: The trust you had with another person was like a house of bricks. One day, you did something, or revealed a whole history of doing something, that essentially blew that house up. All at once, it was gone and you were left with a pile of rubble. Rebuilding trust is like walking over to the pile of bricks and putting them back into a wall one action, one behavior, one day at a time. Sometimes you knock a few off. But as you focus on becoming a trustworthy person, you keep building day-by-day, brick-by-brick. No single action or set of actions will accomplish this, yet actions are very important. As you work on becoming a trustworthy person, keep the following actions in view.

Honor your boundaries; honor her boundaries. By now, you should be developing a list of behaviors and environments that you know to be triggers in your life. These preconditions are minefields leading back into your old behavior, and so you have created boundaries to avoid them. Maybe you have even written a list of these with your spouse. It is absolutely essential that you do everything in your power to uphold these boundaries—*even when you think they are unnecessary*! It is not up to you to decide when you're better and no longer need a guide. Let others make that decision. You and I are too quick to trust ourselves, which leads back into old patterns. Others can help you see when you have changed.

Do what you say you will do in every area of your life. One of the mistakes you can make is to guard your behaviors diligently in one area of life while ignoring others. You may have become more reliable in how you treat the Internet or television. Great. But how are you handling your finances? Are you coming home when you say you will be home? Are you being open and honest about who you text and who you friend on Facebook? Rebuilding trust is far more than avoiding pornography. Rebuilding trust is full-life change. As you become consistently reliable in all areas, trust rebuilds faster.

Stop worrying about looking right. Put your effort into doing right. One temptation you will face when trust starts to rebuild is to hide anything that might jeopardize your progress. Since changing the patterns of behaviors is a two-to-five-year process, along the way you'll inevitably encounter setbacks large and small. It is possible to take this journey without relapsing into pornography itself, but it is not possible to be perfect. You will make mistakes. You will look longer than you should. You will make an error in judgment. You will put yourself first. In these behaviors, you will be tempted to cover over what has happened in order to maintain the trust. Don't! This is only building false trust. You must be totally honest, even in the small areas. Remember: Trust is a result of who you are becoming, not simply what you are doing. Choosing to be honest shows more progress toward you being a trustworthy person than does hiding an indiscretion in hopes of appearing to be trustworthy.

Pour your life into trusting God. If all of this seems like a lot to process, let me encourage you to start here. Devote much time and energy into your relationship with God. Read His story. Discover what He has said about you and what He has promised you. Get friends or your small group to help you do whatever it takes to restore trust in God. As you allow Him to write your identity, it will have a filter-down effect on all your relationships. You don't want your wife or others to trust you just to eliminate the relational discomfort you're feeling. You want them to trust you because you are actually trustworthy! This comes as a direct result of learning to trust God.

THE LINCHPIN: THE BUTTERFLY EFFECT

We can either find our value in our own striving, or we can risk trusting God and find out that He delivers on every promise. Winning the trust of others is a result of who you are, and God alone defines who you are. So stop running and start receiving.

If you took a caterpillar to a scientist who studies the DNA of living creatures, he would make a bold observation. The scientist would tell you that everything in the cells of this bug look and act like those of a butterfly. Even though the critter may currently appear to be a flightless caterpillar, it is in essence a beautiful, winged insect. Because this is true, the caterpillar must become who it already is. The butterfly will emerge.

Written into your spiritual DNA is the fingerprint of God. You have been made in His image and He alone knows your true identity. Though you may currently look or act like a lump of clay, you cannot help but become who you already are. If you will live in confident trust in Christ, you will emerge into your true and trustworthy self.

Rather than striving to behave your way into trust, you can start receiving the identity and value God already has for you. This allows you to live out of a deep place of peace—not the cheap, conflict-avoiding peace of the world, but God's deep and eternal shalom. This shalom involves peace of mind, body, and soul. You don't need to try and change into something or someone you are not; you need to receive the truth of who you already are. God made you. God sees the real you. Will you agree, and see, with Him?

Faith is the confidence that what we hope for will actually happen; it gives us assurance about things we cannot see. Hebrews 11:1

That is why we never give up. Though our bodies are dying, our spirits are being renewed every day. For our present troubles are small and won't last very long. Yet they produce for us a glory that vastly outweighs them and will last forever! So we don't look at the troubles we can see now; rather, we fix our gaze on things that cannot be seen. For the things we see now will soon be gone, but the things we cannot see will last forever. 2 Corinthians 4:16-18

CHAPTER ELEVEN | REBIRTH

At the very end of the Bible, we get a picture of Jesus in Revelation 21. He is coming down from heaven to a new holy city and He proclaims, "Look, I am making everything new!" (Revelation 21:5). While this is a compelling statement, many churches and well-intentioned Christians have built this hope up as something entirely futuristic. This newness that Jesus promises is only in eternity, they teach, at the inauguration of a new heaven and a new earth.

But this is missing the point. Jesus declares with a current, present verb: "I *am* making everything new." He is the one who makes all things new. That's His character. Right now. In this world. Not just when we die and head off into glory, but in our homes and lives now. New marriages, new families, new parents, new hope, new dreams. Jesus actually talked about the Kingdom of God moving in among us, right now. In this place. Experiencing this newness of life will take a shift in the way we do life, which is the subject of this chapter.

We have been on a journey together. We have traveled up the Addictive Path, looking at all the various ways we got trapped by our thinking and our behaviors, even when we didn't mean to. We have emerged onto Breakthrough Peak, where the pain of staying the same was finally greater than the pain of change, and so we chose to die to self and invite real and lasting change into our lives. This critical decision put us onto the Healing Path, where we traveled through true intimacy, community, and identity. We have now arrived at this last chapter of our travels. This would be a good place to stop and ask a fundamental question.

Here it is: "What's the goal here?"

I know, I know. It would seem more sensible to ask this question at the beginning, not the end. But let's be honest; the question we are all asking at the beginning is "How do I get free? How do I stop doing this thing that's ruining me?" We're consumed initially with stopping the bleeding, as we should be. When the initial trauma and shock wears off, though, we need something greater to sustain us. When our relationships return to a place of relative peace and hope, we need a vision strong enough to keep us from drifting back toward old patterns. (Even though the old highways begin to crumble, the brain still knows how to travel that path!)

Our journey from start to finish has been about change, lasting and permanent change. We are not interested in a quick fix or a get-out-of-jail-free card. We long to put to death this old way and pick up a new one. So let's ask the question again: "What's the real goal here?" The goal is to be free of this sin, right? Nope; not even close. That is certainly a desired outcome, but it is only a byproduct of the real goal.

The Apostle Paul heads us down the right path toward an answer when he says, "For you have been called to live in freedom" (Galatians 5:13). Yes, freedom, that's what we want! But freedom for what? What is the purpose, or goal, of this freedom in our day-to-day experience?

Paul goes on: "But don't use your freedom to satisfy your sinful nature." No, we don't want that. We have already found out how attempting to satisfy our sinful nature does nothing to bring real satisfaction. Satisfying our lusts and cravings only leads to imprisonment and bondage. We do not want to walk this whole journey only to leave ourselves open to some new form of slavery. That is what happens to many guys, by the way. With the goal of simply stopping a behavior, they trade one kind of slavery for another. Instead of lust or porn, they take up competition, winning, or some other form of personal satisfaction that is not anymore satisfying than what they had before! We don't want that. A slave master is a slave master no matter what his tactic.

So what's the goal? Paul finishes his thought: "Instead, use your freedom *to serve one another in love*. For the whole law can be summed up in this one command: 'Love your neighbor as yourself'" (Galatians 5:13b-14, italics mine). There it is. The goal of our freedom is that we serve one another in love.

If you're anything like me, this may sound so churchy and religious that the statement comes across as almost meaningless. We know that loving others is good, healthy, and the right thing to do, but it hardly seems inspiring as a life goal, right? We are like the little boy in Sunday school, who, when the teacher asked, "What is brown, furry, and stores up nuts for the winter?" answered, "Well, I know the answer is Jesus, but it sure sounds like a squirrel to me!" We have learned that loving and serving is the right answer, but this doesn't do much for us. So let me expound on the idea.

The first six to eight months of this journey were extremely eye-opening for me. I was on a steep and rapid growth curve. The pain was intense, but so was the newly found freedom and hope. Every week I received some kind of revelation about myself, about my past patterns, and about what needed to change in my heart. The deepest of these revelations was a continuing thread about the depth of my addiction to self and to feeling good. I realized my whole life was centered around making myself look and feel good.

I reflected on this one Sunday morning as I walked through our church auditorium before the worship service. I remember saying, "What now, Lord? If it's not all about me, why I am here? I have done this for me and my glory for so long that I am not sure what else will motivate me." It was a humbling, but very true, admission. I was in it for the crowd, the recognition, and the success. Sure, Jesus and faith and love were in there too, but I was truly driven by self. I had geared my life so tightly around self that I was not sure how else to live.

In the quiet of that morning, a new thought came into my mind. I don't always know how God speaks or when it is God, but in looking back I can only say this word felt divine. The answer I heard that morning was, "Love. You can actually love them for Me, and not just for what they can do for you. Love will motivate you." I was moved to tears to realize that I was finally free to do what I had been called to do all along. Love and serve the bride of Christ, His church, for the glory of the Groom, Christ Himself.

Only one time in His earthly ministry did Jesus give the disciples a commandment. Certainly, much of what He said was in command form and He fully expected His word to be followed, but only once did He use the words, "This is my command." Jesus said, "So now I am giving you a new commandment: Love each other. Just as I have loved you, you should love each other" (John 13:34). He's so intent on the disciples getting this (they did tend to be a bit thick-headed) that He repeated it two more times in the sermon (John 15:12, 17). But this wasn't new. The Old Testament book of Leviticus, written some two thousand years earlier, had instructed the people to love their neighbors as themselves. But Jesus continued, "Just as I have loved you, you should love each other." That was new.

You see, the idea that Jesus, the Teacher, Lord, and Messiah, should serve, wash feet, and love His followers like brothers and friends was unheard of in that society. But Jesus says that the model for love is His life. Jesus' life mission was to become our life mission.

Our journey toward freedom must become one of serving and loving others. We remove ourselves from the center; rather than allowing a new addiction or obsession to move in, we make a life of love our goal.

When this process began for me in February of 2010, I thought I had a "problem" with pornography, but the rest of my life was essentially pretty good. What I have discovered at every single turn is that pornography was the symptom of much deeper struggles in my heart. I had developed an addiction to porn, yes; but this came about long after other unholy obsessions: competing and comparing myself to others, pursuing the glory of my name and my success, and putting my wants and needs above those of everyone else in my world. As I have addressed my weakness with pornography, God has graciously taken me into a new place in all these other areas as well.

This path, while difficult and painful at times, has been so worth it. Over a five-year period, I spent $25,000 and countless hours away from my family to earn a Master of Divinity degree from a leading university. But this Pure Desire journey has changed me far more than seminary ever did because it forced me to find out what was going on in my heart. Rather than simply adding knowledge and information, this journey has revolved around true transformation.

Several months into my meetings with Dr. Ted Roberts, he was praying for me after one of our sessions. He spoke these words that struck me so powerfully that I wrote them down. In a moment of divine inspiration, he prayed (and I quote), "Nick, the revelation you seek will come as you teach others and train them." At the time, the words felt a little foreign because I was mainly focused on changing myself, and to be honest, I didn't really want to tell others about the mistakes I had made. But over the last few years, I have watched the truth of these words play out in my life.

While I am definitely a work in progress, I am discovering the mystery of self-fulfillment (Christ in me!) that comes from focusing my life on others. In 1 Corinthians 3, Paul says that in the scheme of salvation, he really isn't all that important as a man. He simply "did the work the Lord gave [him]" (v. 5). I have found that I am free to do the God-given work of serving others and God instead of competing and comparing myself to the work and accomplishments of others. Rather than pursuing my name and my success, I can look for His glory to be revealed. In the words of John the Baptist: "He must become greater and greater, and I must become less and less" (John 3:30). Liberation is to stop worrying about getting what's coming to me and focus my efforts on the needs of others. This is the true meaning of Philippians 2:3b: "Be humble, thinking of others as better than yourselves."

You will never experience ultimate and lasting freedom until this journey ceases to be about you and becomes all about others around you. You are being set free in order to serve others. At birth, we learn that the world revolves around us. It must! As infants, our needs are the only needs that matter. Maturity is an ongoing process of discovering that life is about others. This is rebirth—a new heaven, a new earth, and a new us!

GOD'S STORY: THE GREAT "IN ORDER THAT…"

The Bible so beautifully illustrates all of this for us. Let me give you four brief examples of how this kind of living—living to serve others—is integral to the Kingdom of God. This isn't a new idea at all; this is what God had in mind from the beginning!

ABRAHAM

In Genesis 12, God selected a man named Abram, whose name was later changed to Abraham, to be the recipient of a great blessing. He told Abraham to leave his native land and head off to a place that God would show him. There, God promised Abraham he would become a great nation. He would be famous in all the earth. God said the reason He chose to bless Abraham and make his descendants into a mighty nation was so that he can bless everyone else.

If God came to us and promised to bless our family, what kind of images come to mind for us? We imagine, perhaps, a large house, smarter-than-average children, and a peaceful, joyful existence. Very Garrison Keillor, Lake Wobegon kind of imagery! We are blessed, we think, in order to enjoy the blessing. This, however, is an Americanized, consumerized version of a true, godly blessing. God blesses us in order that we might bless others.

DAVID

The book of 2 Samuel tells the story of David's sin with Bathsheba. He looked, he lusted, he laid, he lied, he lured Uriah to his death, and he lamented. The prophet Nathan confronted David with his sin (2 Samuel 12), and David did not fail to confess. He owned his mistake and threw himself on the mercy of God. It is in the book of Psalms that we get an inside look at David's personal confession. Psalm 51 is subtitled, "A psalm of David regarding the time Nathan the prophet came to him after David had committed adultery with Bathsheba." While this may be a fairly lengthy title for a song, it gives us an exact situation for his words.

Some of Psalm 51 might be familiar to you. Verses 10-12 were turned into a nifty, over-sung chorus in the early 80s:

"Create in me a clean heart, O God. And renew a right spirit within me. Cast me not away from your presence, O Lord, and take not your Holy Spirit from me. Restore unto me the joy of thy salvation, and renew a right spirit within me." Ah, the memories come flooding back to me of Sunday night sing-a-longs and the faithful grandmas, vibratos and all, singing loudly in the pew behind me.

While the words to this chorus were familiar to me, the following verse was not. Do you know verse 13? This passage is often overlooked in favor of the much more famous couplets that precede it. But I think the heart of this psalm is here. After the well-known words, David goes on to say, "Then I will teach your ways to rebels, and they will return to you."

Isn't that beautiful? David looks at everything he is asking from God—a clean slate, a fresh start, forgiveness—and proclaims that the purpose for all of this is serving others. David is saying, "God, when You forgive and restore me, I will teach others how to be restored as well." God forgives us in order that we may lead others into forgiveness as well.

PETER

In the Gospel of Luke, Jesus has unique words for His disciple Peter: "Simon, Simon, Satan has asked to sift each of you like wheat" (Luke 22:31). Jesus was referring to the coming days when all of Peter's dreams and expectations for Jesus would be shattered. Peter would deny Christ to a mere servant girl. Instead of watching Jesus ride triumphantly through Jerusalem as a conquering hero, Peter would see Jesus stumble His way down the street with a cross on His shoulders. His Messiah would die. This is the sifting of Peter's faith that was about to happen. Jesus saw it. Jesus knew how Peter would run away from Him and deny Him.

But then this ray of hope: "When you have repented and turned to me again, strengthen and build up your brothers." Jesus gave a prophetic word about the restoration of Peter, focusing on the idea that his restoration would be for the benefit of his brothers, his fellow disciples.

These words were echoed at the Sea of Galilee where Jesus found Peter fishing again. His thrice-repeated question to Peter was, "Do you love me?" When Peter responded each time in the affirmative, while growing increasingly adamant, "Yes Lord, you know that I do!" what did Jesus call him to do? "Go and feed my sheep." In other words, Jesus told Peter that the way he could show his devotion to Christ was to go and take care of—go and serve—the people of Christ. Jesus restored Peter and commissioned him to go and serve others. His goal is the same in restoring you and me.

US

"This is all well and good," you might say, "but I'm not a Bible hero. The people in those pages are there for a reason; they had great faith. I'm not sure I stack up with them. Isn't it enough for me to just focus on my recovery?" I understand exactly where you're coming from. You have wanted to be free for so long that just achieving this goal seems more than enough. Why complicate it all with ideas about ministering to and serving others?

Here's why: *You are not trying to change a behavior, but to transform your way of doing life.* Lust, pornography, or whatever is tripping you up is a symptom of deeper things. Those deeper things change when our perspective moves off of ourselves and onto others.

Paul voices this nicely for us in Colossians 3. He writes some of my favorite words here: "You have been raised to new life with Christ" (Colossians 3:1); "For you died to this life, and your real life is hidden with Christ in God" (Colossians 3:3); "So put to death the sinful, earthly things lurking within you" (Colossians 3:5). Paul proclaims that we have been given a glorious new life in Christ, and because of this, we must "put to death" the old and put on the new. God has made us new, so be clothed in this new life! Get all geared up and declare, "This is the new me! What do you think? Ta-da!"

Be clothed. Clothe yourself in the new. But why? For us? No! Look at the garments we are to put on. Tenderhearted mercy—toward others! Kindness—toward others! Humility, gentleness, and patience—all of these can only be done with and for others. Go ahead and try to live this list out in isolation. Impossible! You are to "make allowance for each other's faults and forgive anyone who offends you. Remember, the Lord forgave you, so you must forgive others. Above all, clothe yourselves with love, which binds us all together in perfect harmony" (Colossians 3:13-14). Everything new that Paul tells us we are to put on is a way of life wrapped up in the needs and interests of others. We strip off the old, self-glorifying ways in order that we might be clothed in servant robes for others.

God has blessed, forgiven, commissioned, and renewed us *in order that* we might bless, forgive, commission, and renew others in His Spirit. You are set free for the world. I love the vision statement of a church I visited recently in Portland, Oregon. Their motto states, "We exist to follow Jesus in authentic community *for the world*." They are bold enough to say that everything they do as a church is not actually for them, but for the world outside the church community. Imagine how the church in America would be reshaped if this were the heart's cry of every congregation! It's not for us, but for the world. Grasping this principle is absolutely key to walking in true freedom.

OUR STORY: LEAVING A LEGACY

What legacy do you want to pass on? When you get right down to it, we have a strong desire as men to build something worth passing on to those who will come behind us. A business, a church, a family, a way of life—we want to look back on what we have done and see that it is good and stands the test of time.

I want you to see that the legacy you leave is completely wrapped up in this decision to serve others. Because the truth is, no matter what you're doing—running a business, working your way through school, or serving at a church—someone is watching you. They are watching not just what you do, but the *way* you do it.

Who is watching you and the way you handle sin and weakness in your life? If you have a son, he's watching. I don't care what his age, his temperament or his faith situation might be; he's watching. You can pass on all of the money, IRAs, or business you want, but these things will mean far less to him than what you model in areas of integrity, humility, and honesty through which you pass on blessings or curses.

Others are watching. Your daughter is defining manhood by watching you. Your wife is learning about unconditional love by watching you. Those who don't know Christ are watching in order to decide what it means to be a Christian. Your neighbors are watching the way you live, even in the small areas like how you put out your garbage or talk to the postman. I guarantee you, someone is watching.

What is the message that you're declaring to all of these lives? You will communicate one of two messages. On the one hand, you can live in such a way that says to others, "Life is all about me." You can spend your days building your image by pursuing success and wealth. You can believe that somehow leaving all of this to others is a benevolent move. In truth, the message they will pick up on is self-centeredness. Those you influence will make life all about themselves, too!

On the other hand, you can live in such a way as to say, in as many ways as possible, "Life is all about Jesus, and you are more important than me." You can spend your hours and moments loving, giving, and sacrificing for others. You may or may not end up with much physical wealth or accumulation to show for it, but that's okay. They don't really want your money; others around you want to know how to live well. And as you live to serve, so also will they.

Can you imagine what would happen if the church today began to produce a new generation of men? What if we were that new generation? Not trapped by secrecy and sexual sin, but able to be authentic about struggle and then walk in victory. Not addicted to self-aggrandizement and success, but dedicated to the success and wellbeing of others. Not running to build our empire, but passionate to see the Kingdom of God lived out among us. What could that generation do for the world?

What if our sons saw a different path through sexuality than the immoral, visually explicit babe-fest thrown at them daily by our sex-crazed culture? What if our sons watched us and saw that it was okay to be real about our desires and urges, and what if our sons knew there was a healthy way to handle them? What if our sons watched how to confess in humility, receive true forgiveness, and be empowered to live differently? I think a bit of a new heaven and a new earth would begin right here.

We must have a passionate, consuming vision of what God wants to do not just in us, but also through us. This is the final step to freedom. A consuming vision for changing your life got you on this journey, and a consuming vision for using your life to help others change is what keeps you on it! I know that a guy really "gets it" on this journey when he stops caring about how his behaviors are affecting him and looks at what his behaviors do to others. When he sees that everything he does—good or bad— influences others, he picks up the key to become transformed into the image and likeness of Christ! We can either make life about us and be stuck in places of pain and sin, or we can make life about others and discover the freeing way God has for us.

YOU LEAVE A POWERFUL LEGACY WHEN YOU DO THE FOLLOWING THINGS:

SERVE YOUR WIFE BEFORE YOU SERVE YOURSELF

Serving others must start as close to home as possible. Nothing will impact your children more than to watch their dad love their mom through acts of service. Find out what she needs, and do it! Does she need help with the dishes? The laundry? Maybe you don't even know where your kids' clothes go. Find out. You can do this. You can take apart a car engine or write computer software; I know you can separate lights from darks. As men, we put up a lot of excuses for not helping more. But most of these excuses are simply rooted in a desire to be served rather than to serve. Are you using the best of yourself—your time, energy, and talents—to serve your wife, or does she get the leftovers? If you cannot serve your wife, you cannot serve the world.

TREAT YOUR CHILDREN AS PEOPLE, NOT POSSESSIONS

Many men think their job with the kids is roughly the same as their job with the car. Keep the gas tank full, get the oil changed, and protect the body from unnecessary damage. Feed them, change them, clothe them, and take care of them until they head out the door. The problem with this way of parenting is the failure to see our children as human beings with real emotions, problems, and fears. You serve your children when you get in touch with them as fellow human beings. Take them out for ice cream and find out what worries them. Listen to their stories and ramblings to find out what really drives their thoughts and emotions. Look them in the eye and show them you value them as equals. Take them seriously.

I recently heard a speaker say that he and his wife had always chosen to invest more money in experiences than possessions for their kids. This rang true with me. In looking back at my childhood, I see that I now care very little about the kind of dresser I had, the type of car my parents drove, or the size of house we lived in. What I remember are the experiences like summer camp, family vacations, and big holiday celebrations. Those moments shaped me, while the possessions were mere props on the set. Invest in building your kids through outstanding family experiences!

GET INVOLVED IN YOUR LOCAL CHURCH

A fascinating study was released a few years ago that reported on a person's church attendance based on the father and mother's practices.[30] The study found that if a mother is regularly involved in church, but the father is not, about sixty percent of their children drift away from church. However, if the father is a regular church attendee, but the mother is not, that number drops in half, to roughly thirty percent. This percentage is even lower if both a mother and father are regularly involved in church! What does this mean? Well, it does not mean that Mom should stay home from church. What it means is that as Dad goes, so the children go. When you serve in your local church, you make a definitive life statement about what matters most. Find the place where you fit and go for it!

SHARE YOUR STORY OF ADDICTION AND FREEDOM

This may be the primary place where your healing is not about you. Realize that if you have found freedom from sexual addiction and pornography, you are in a small minority of men in this world. Reports now are saying that as much as seventy percent of men visit pornographic websites at least monthly. The struggle is not rare, but the ability to talk about it and find real victory are still rare. Look for opportunities to be real with other men and you will see God do amazing things through you. Like David, God is restoring a new spirit in you *in order that* you can teach His ways to others who are trapped.

TALK TO STRANGERS LIKE FAMILY

Your daily interaction with the world around you provides prime opportunities to display the change of Christ in your life. You may not get to share any of your story or talk about God, but you can be Christ in the smallest of ways. Look the cashier in the eye and use her name when you say thanks. Be respectful and kind to the waiter who messes up your order. Be polite while waiting in line. Express empathy for the airline attendant dealing with a tough flight. Jesus said, "But I say, love your enemies!…If you love only those who love you, what reward is there in that?…If you are kind only to your friends, how are you different from anyone else?" (Matthew 5:44,46-47). The barista handing out your coffee probably isn't your enemy, but treating her with love and respect communicates to others the change God has brought into your life.

DO GOOD IN YOUR COMMUNITY & NEIGHBORHOOD

The New Testament book of Acts says: "And you know that God anointed Jesus of Nazareth with the Holy Spirit and with power. Then Jesus went around *doing good* and healing all who were oppressed by the devil, for God was with him" (Acts 10:38, italics mine). Of all that Jesus did in this world, we often miss that fact that He simply *did good*. Others watched how He loved, served, and healed; through this they learned about God.

As followers of Christ, we can become overly focused on being good. This is what we learned through our Sunday school years—go into the world and be a good little boy. But not enough emphasis was placed on going out to do good, which reveals the loving works of the Father.

IT'S TOO LATE FOR ME!

As you read this chapter, you may have found yourself thinking these very words. The place you are in life is too far advanced to undo the problems and trouble you have created. Serving others and giving your life away is a nice idea for a younger man.

This makes me think of some advice I read from Ann Landers many, many years ago. No, I don't often read Ann Landers, but for some reason this article was passed my way. An older gal had written to ask some advice about life, saying she was very interested in becoming a doctor. Her drawback was that after the eight years of training this would require, she would be sixty-four. Ann's response to her was genius: "How old will you be in eight years if you don't become a doctor?" In other words, if you don't do the thing you have on your heart to do, you will still be sixty-four! Might as well get there doing what you feel called and led to do.

How old will you be if you don't change? It's never too late to start becoming the person God made you to be. Time will pass by whether you sit back and watch or devote yourself to something new.

I love the Apostle Paul's heart. At the end of the book of Romans, which most everyone agrees was written later in his life, he makes this statement: "But now I have finished my work in these [other] regions, and after all these long years of waiting, I am eager to visit you. I am planning to go to Spain, and when I do, I will stop off in Rome" (Romans 15:23-24). We don't know exactly what Paul planned to do in Spain, but we can determine with a fair amount of certainty that Paul had never been there before. He likely didn't know the language, the culture, or the people. But God had put the mission on his heart, and he was making plans to go!

By this time, he had planted churches all over a great part of the known world. He could have said, "Now I have finished my work and I am planning to go home and take it easy." Instead, his eyes are on the next frontier. You may have finished one season or several seasons of life, but could this be your next frontier? You are never too old to start living out God's dream for your life.

LINCHPIN: THE JOURNEY IS THE DESTINATION

An old car commercial depicts a father walking into the room of a screaming baby. He scoops up the little guy in his arms and carries him down to the garage, where he places the boy lovingly in the back seat of his car. The father drives slowly through the neighborhood in his sleek, new sedan while the baby is calmed and eventually lulled to sleep by the smooth, rhythmic ride. As the father pulls back into the garage and heads upstairs to lay his son gently back in bed, a voice-over comes on and says, "The journey *is* the destination."

As we reach the end of our journey together, I remind you of the same idea. This "destination" is only the beginning of a new journey. Our goal has been to bust free from the prison of pornography, but as this liberation occurs, we discover that the real journey has just begun. Rather than living out a self-focused existence, we are released to serve others and enter into all that God has for us.

I am discovering that change is less about "that one moment" and more about the process. This process could be summed up with the refrain from John the Baptist, "I must become less and less, and He must become greater and greater."

Will you make this choice? Will you choose to use your freedom, not as an opportunity to indulge your selfish ambitions, but to serve others in love? Author Hans Kung says this well: "To be able to do what one wants is only the appearance of freedom; true freedom is to will what God does."[31] Being free to "do as we please" is only the illusion of freedom, while doing life God's way brings true liberation. That kind of freedom is a destination, a journey, worthy of our life.

AFTERWORD

Multnomah Falls, near Portland, Oregon, is one of the most scenic and beautiful places in our country and one of my favorite places to run. This falls has a walking path that ascends nearly one mile from the base parking lot to the very top of the falls where you can step out on a small observation deck for a fantastic panoramic view of the Columbia River Gorge as the falls thunders beneath your feet. Most of the crowd stops here. What they don't know is that some of the most awesome, pristine landscape is to be found in the miles past this point. Many more waterfalls and a plethora of forested beauty await those who venture onward.

I love running up there; I feel for a few moments like I am the only person in the world, back in the perfect Garden of Eden. On this particular day, it had been some time since I'd been up the winding trail to the top of the falls. I parked my car and began jogging the switchback ascent toward my eagerly awaited wilderness. What I had forgotten was the steepness and length of the ascent. After what seemed like a dozen switchbacks, I thought to myself, *I must be nearly there!* At that moment, I came around a turn in the trail and noticed a signpost. In bright green and white, this small plaque declared, "Switchback 5 of 11."

"You have got to be kidding me!" I literally yelled out loud to no one in particular. My legs were spent and my lungs were tired. I longed for the great expanse that waited at the top, but I suddenly doubted my ability to get there. But what choice did

I have? So I kept trudging forward as the signposts continued to mark my slow, yet steady progress.

You may be in a similar place as you conclude this book. In your struggle with sexual sin, you have fought hard. You have rounded many corners and keep looking up, wondering if you're near the top. But then something occurs—a setback, an argument, a relapse into old thinking and old behaving—and all the vigor drains from your legs or your soul. You wonder if you will ever get to this wonderful place of freedom and get beyond the pain.

I believe that our journey has some signposts along the way. As I conclude, let me give you five of them. If you find yourself passing these plaques on your run to freedom, be encouraged. You are making progress, and you will reach your final goal.

HOW DO YOU KNOW IF YOU'VE STARTED THE JOURNEY?

1) HAVE YOU FACED THE DEPTH OF YOUR STRUGGLE?

Have you admitted to yourself, and to others, that this problem is bigger than your ability to figure it out? As long as we hold onto the flawed notion that we can handle this ourselves, we will not be free. If you have looked in the mirror and said, "I have a problem, and I don't know how to fix it" you have made progress. If you have looked others in the eye and said the same thing, mark this turn off the list. You are well along the path to freedom.

2) ARE YOU TRULY INVITING OTHERS IN?

Who else knows about this struggle in your life? If the only person is your spouse, you're in a real danger zone. She cannot be the one to help you find freedom. Not alone. Do other trusted and respected men know of this struggle? And more importantly, are they involved in your life in a regular, intentional way? Let me say again that for a dozen years, I confessed this sin to numerous godly men, but change did not occur because these men were not an ongoing part of my story. A weekly Pure Desire group changed my life because I was no longer alone. Who do you have?

Our temptation is to work harder, figure it out and not bother others with our problems. I would ask you as it was asked of me, "How's that working for you?" It has been said that many Christians are self-conscious, but most are not self-aware. We worry about what others think of us, but we do little to see ourselves. Self-awareness comes through our willingness to invite others into our life in a deep way.

3) DO YOU ENGAGE CHANGE ON MULTIPLE LEVELS?

As I have tried to highlight throughout the book, lasting change will not occur if you focus only on modifying behaviors. Change is the result of new behaviors, strengthened beliefs, and a transformed brain. New behaviors are the result of establishing healthy boundaries and practices in your life. Beliefs are strengthened as you study God's Word and allow other men and teachers to help you apply His truth to your life. Your brain is transformed through new positive experiences in how you handle pain and the stresses of life. If you look around your life at the steps you're currently taking and can identify steps in all three of these areas, you're making steady progress!

4) IS YOUR IDENTITY GROUNDED IN CHRIST ALONE?

At the core of your struggle with pornography or sexuality is a misplaced identity. Whether through our family of origin or past negative experiences, we have developed unhealthy ways of defining who we are. Performance, success, humor, possessions, relationships, and accomplishment can all be alternative ways of defining who we are. While some of these may be good and valuable, nothing in our life outside of the Creator can fully define us. In your journey, you will learn to strip off the false self in order to get to the core of who God has made you to be.

5) HAS YOUR FOCUS MOVED BEYOND SELF?

Are you in this for you, or are you truly committed to others? As Dr. Ted Roberts has said, "You'll know you've turned a corner when you realize how much you have hurt others." When you see the pain you have caused others, you are motivated to change. This motivation will lead you into a way of life defined by serving others and caring about their needs.

HONESTLY SPEAKING…

While I hope that something in this book has helped you gain real footholds for change in your journey, my greater hope is that some of these words will start to shift the approach our churches have toward lust, pornography, and sexual sin. The truth is: Sexual sin in our culture is developing much faster than our ability to fight it. We need to stop fighting the battle of telling the culture how bad it is and focus on the war for men's hearts. I will be very grateful if this book infuses energy into the battle for men's hearts within the church.

I believe that unless churches change their approach to helping men deal with sexual struggles, the church will be irrelevant in fifteen years. A whole generation of men will grow up and see church as the one place where they cannot talk about what may be the most pervasive desire in their life. Without freedom to be honest, they will process this journey alone. As we have seen over and over, any choice for isolation in this battle guarantees defeat. The church must become a place of hope and healing for men who are trapped! The church must teach men to talk to their sons, and sons to talk to their fathers. Alone we are crushed, but together we can destroy this beast. When we begin winning the war for men's hearts, the cultural battle will begin to shift as well.

My church is just starting this journey, but I know we have made solid progress. Since sharing our journey with the church in the spring of 2011, my wife and I have watched both men and women walk through healing and into recovery in change groups. These groups are multiplying and are being facilitated by those who have walked the path themselves. New people are jumping in, and men and women who wanted little to do with the church before are now finding it's relevant after all.

I have had more difficult, honest conversations in the last year than in my previous ten years of ministry, but these are the right conversations. In the past, I always felt a couple would come in eight to ten years later than they needed the help. By then, the marriage or the truth was so far gone that repair was difficult if not impossible. Now we are helping people on the front end of this journey and releasing them into new hope and freedom.

This has been a realization of God's dream for our church. We have prayed and longed for authenticity and breakthrough in people's lives. Little did I know that these things had to happen in my life first so they could be released into the lives of many others.

God is up to the same business in your life. He is doing something in you right now that is the fulfillment of your dreams for your marriage, your family, and your life. The journey may not always feel that way, but you can trust that God is good and that He is for you. He is in this for your good and for His glory.

If you have read this far, I have to say thank you. Thank you for believing that I had something worth saying and for sticking with it to the end. Far more importantly, thank you for believing in yourself. Thank you for believing that you are a person worthy of God's liberating power to do great things in your life. Through every page and chapter, I hope that this is the message you have heard over and over: God values you so much that He will do anything to bring freedom and hope into your life, including dying on a cross to cover all your shame and give you the power to become a new creation.

When Jesus promised that you would be free, He meant it. I have begun to experience that freedom in a real way, and I believe with all my heart that you will too.

RESOURCES

PURE DESIRE MINISTRIES INTERNATIONAL
GRESHAM, OR | WWW.PUREDESIRE.ORG | 503.489.0230
Pure Desire Ministries, led by Dr. Ted Roberts and Diane Roberts, has practical answers that deal not only with the struggle of sexual and other addictions, but also with the family systems that fuel the issues.

RESOURCES AVAILABLE INCLUDE:
Seven Pillars of Freedom Men's Workbook by Dr. Ted Roberts

Top Gun: Flight Manual for Young Men in a Pornified World by Dr. Ted Roberts & Bryan Roberts

Betrayal & Beyond: Healing for Broken Trust Workbooks I, II, and III by Diane Roberts

Eight Pillars to Freedom from Love Addiction & Sexual Issues Workbooks I and II by Diane Roberts

Behind the Mask: Authentic Living for Young Women by Rebecca Bradley & Diane Roberts

Hope for Men: Healing for Broken Trust by Ted & Diane Roberts

Pure Desire (The Book) by Dr. Ted Roberts

THE GENESIS PROCESS FOR CHANGE GROUPS BY MICHAEL DYE
WWW.GENESISPROCESS.ORG
The Genesis Process will help you understand how your addictions have affected your life and relationships and give you some basic recovery principles and practical tools to bring about biblically based life change.

BIBLIOGRAPHY

de Mello, Anthony. Edited by Stroud, J. Francis, S. J. de Mello. *Awareness: A de Mello Spirituality Conference in His Own Words.* New York: Image Books/Doubleday, 1992.

Driscoll, Mark, and Grace Driscoll. *Real Marriage: The Truth About Sex, Friendship & Life Together.* Nashville: Thomas Nelson, 2012.

Dye, Michael. *The Genesis Process for Change Groups, Book 1 & Book 2.* Auburn, CA: Michael Dye, 2006. www.genesisprocess.org.

MacDonald, Gordon. *When Men Think Private Thoughts.* Nashville: Thomas Nelson, 1996.

Roberts, Ted. *Pure Desire: How One Man's Triumph Can Help Others Break Free from Sexual Temptation.* 2nd ed. Ventura, CA: Regal Books, 2008.

Roberts, Ted. *Seven Pillars of Freedom Men's Workbook.* Gresham, OR: Pure Desire Ministries International, 2010.

Struthers, William M. *Wired for Intimacy: How Pornography Hijacks the Male Brain.* Downers Grove, IL: IVP Books, 2009.

Wilkerson, Mike. *Redemption: Freed by Jesus from the Idols We Worship and the Wounds We Carry.* Wheaton, IL: Crossway, 2011.

ENDNOTES

[1] Anthony de Mello. Edited by Stroud, J. Francis, S. J. De Mello, *Awareness: A de Mello Spirituality Conference in His Own Words* (New York: Image Books/Doubleday, 1992) Chapter 7.

[2] Ibid.

[3] Dr. Ted Roberts. *Seven Pillars of Freedom Men's Workbook* (Gresham, OR: Pure Desire Ministries International, 2010) 63.

[4] Mark & Grace Driscoll. *Real Marriage: The Truth About Sex, Friendship, and Life Together* (Nashville, TN: Thomas Nelson, 2012) Chapter 6.

[5] *The Lord of the Rings: The Fellowship of the Ring.* New Line Home Entertainment, 2001.

[6] Dietrich Bonhoeffer. *Life Together* (New York: Harper One, 1954) 110.

[7] Dr. Omar Minwalla, Licensed Psychologist & Clinical Sexologist. http://www.theinstituteforsexualhealth. com/staff/omar-minwalla-psy-d/ ; http:// understandinghersideofthestory.com/The Sexual Trauma Model.html. 2008.

[8] Mike Wilkerson. *Redemption: Freed by Jesus from the Idols We Worship and the Wounds We Carry* (Wheaton, IL: Crossway, 2011) e-book, from the Introduction.

[9] Dr. Ted Roberts. *Seven Pillars of Freedom Men's Workbook* (Gresham, OR: Pure Desire Ministries International, 2010) 90.

[10] Bill Thrall, Bruce McNicol & John Lynch. *True Faced* (Colorado Springs, CO: NavPress, 2004).

[11] Thrall, McNicol, & Lynch. *True Faced*. 55.

[12] C. S. Lewis. *The Great Divorce* (New York: Macmillan, 1946).

[13] C. S. Lewis. *The Weight of Glory*.

[14] Dr. Ted Roberts. *Seven Pillars of Freedom Men's Workbook* (Gresham, OR: Pure Desire Ministries International, 2010) From Pillar of Freedom 3 Lesson One by Harry Flanagan. 104.

[15] Anthony de Mello, Edited by Stroud, J. Francis, S. J. de Mello. *Awareness: A de Mello Spirituality Conference in His Own Words* (New York: Image Books/Doubleday, 1992).

[16] Mark and Grace Driscoll. *Real Marriage: The Truth About Sex, Friendship, and Life Together* (Nashville, TN: Thomas Nelson, 2012) Chapter 8.

[17] Ibid. Chapter 6.

[18] FASTER Scale. Michael Dye. *The Genesis Process for Change Groups, Book 2* (Auburn, CA: Michael Dye, 2006) www.genesisprocess.org.

[19] Simon Tugwell. *A Prayer*. Reproduced in *A Guide to Prayer for Ministers and Other Servants* by Job & Shawchuck (Nashville, TN: Upper Room Books, 1993).

[20] Harvey & Lois Seifert. *Liberation of Life*. As quoted in A *Guide to Prayer for Ministers and Other Servants* by Job & Shawchuck (Nashville, TN: Upper Room Books, 1993).

[21] Statistics from "The Human Brain: God's Design" video, www.godtube.com.

[22] Dr. Ted Roberts. *Seven Pillars of Freedom Men's Workbook* (Gresham, OR: Pure Desire Ministries International, 2010) 56.

[23] The *Seven Pillars of Freedom Workbook* gives a detailed account of the various parts of the brain and how they function in creating these pathways of addiction. See pages 23-35. Don't dismiss these pages as pointless anatomy. Understanding God's creation of your brain is incredibly effective in helping to rewire it for change!

[24] To view the FASTER Scale, see *The Genesis Process for Change Groups, Book 2* (Auburn, CA: Michael Dye, 2006) www.genesisprocess.org. Chapter 5.

[25] Michael Dye. *Genesis Process for Change Groups, Book 1* (Auburn, CA: Michael Dye, 2006) www.genesisprocess.org. Chapter 4.

[26] Gordon MacDonald. *When Men Think Private Thoughts* (Nashville: Thomas Nelson, 1996).

[27] Dr. Ted Roberts. *Seven Pillars of Freedom Men's Workbook* (Gresham, OR: Pure Desire Ministries International, 2010) 40.

[28] Diane Roberts. *Betrayal & Beyond Workbook II* (Gresham, OR: Pure Desire Ministries International, 2010) Pillar 6, Lesson Three.

[29] Dr. Ted Roberts. *Seven Pillars of Freedom Men's Workbook* (Gresham, OR: Pure Desire Ministries International, 2010) 62.

[30] *The Truth About Men & Church: On the Importance of Fathers to Churchgoing.* Robbie Low. http://trushare.com/83APR02/AP02LOW.htm.

[31] Job & Shawchuck. *A Guide to Prayer for Ministers and Other Servants* (Nashville, TN: Upper Room Books, 1993) 192.